The **Annoyed** Voter's Guide

To 2014 & 2015

Anthony Wilcox

CreateSpace Publishing

Copyright © by CreateSpace Independent Publishing Platform

All rights reserved. No part of this book may be transmitted in any form by any means without permission in writing from the publisher.

Printed in the U.S.A.

First Printing: October 2014

Printed on acid-free, recycled paper

ISBN-13: 978-1502761552

ISBN-10: 1502761556

CreateSpace Independent Publishing Platform

www.CreateSpace.com

Contents

3

Dedicated to the memories of James Foley and Steven Sotloff, and their families.

Great journalism is often inspired by a hatred of injustice, and sustained by both personal strength and courage. It is delivered, with an altruistic spirit, to attempt to satisfy one's relentless appetite for the pursuit of truth, and the conveyance of reality. The passion, bravery, and self-sacrifice both men displayed are at the heart of what makes responsive democracy possible, and their legacies live on.

Preface

Give to us clear vision that we may know where to stand, and what to stand for— because unless we stand for something, we shall fall for anything.

-Peter Marshall, U.S. Senate Chaplain, April 18, 1947

Before we venture too deeply into what can quickly become the quicksand of American electoral politics, I want to answer a few questions that you, being the bright and questioning reader you are, surely have burning deep down inside. The first of these most likely resembles "Who do this jerk think he is?" followed closely by the consequently justifiable, "Why should I care anyway?"

Well, to tell the truth, I come to you as both a humble fellow citizen, and a concerned American voter, who genuinely wonders where this country is heading in the near-and-also-distant future. As a matter of full disclosure, I grew up in a pretty standard middle-class household in the Midwest. My family tended to lean a little Democratic, which was and still is sort of an anomaly in our red-stained capital city, located in central Illinois. My first recollection of politics was watching CNN with my grandfather as a kid, and deciding to announce that I owed zero allegiance to either the "Dumb-o-crats" or the "Re-poop-lick-ans," and would focus my serious energy towards watching and playing baseball.

But I eventually became nerdily-engrossed in politics at the age of 14, when in 2000, George W. Bush somehow ended up President of the United States, instead of Al Gore, despite receiving fewer popular votes nationally. The ensuing battle (or lack thereof), got me interested in why something as important as this could play out, on the national stage no less, in a way that seemed to make so little sense. Unfortunately, the Bush years would be full of these perplexing, but all-too-common, "Are we really doing that?" policy decisions and moments. Luckily for my generation, Jon Stewart was there to make it all feel at least a little wittier and

7

funnier, by talking about important political events in a way that both entertained and informed people; which, by the way, I feel is the quickest path to re-energizing American citizenship and political participation. I am proud to say that I never bought into the reasoning given behind the War in Iraq, despite being surrounded by a bunch of Bush-loving hawks in my Catholic high school. I cast my first Presidential election ballot for John Kerry in 2004, and struggled to accept his defeat the day after. But my interest in politics has never felt like it could be fully expressed through the overzealous and mindless support of "one side."

I think it's the truth when people claim that everyone involved in politics, practiced in its many ways, has that one moment that they can look back to, which served as their motivation for getting involved in what basically amounts to a big, egotistical, and yes, even important, fight over who gets what. The interesting part about American politics is that there are so many potential angles to take: some people decide they have to run for office, some marry themselves to a cause or candidate they deem worth their effort, while others just want to wear a suit and spend way too much money on hair products (and not surprisingly, are most often the ones in it for the thrill of obtaining power, or money, or both). And others, who feel too put-off to really be involved in this fracas, typically end up teaching classes, or writing about it.

I suppose my moment occurred in 2005, when I accompanied my dad and a friend to see Christopher Hitchens speak at Illinois State University, as a part of his book tour for his then-recently released biography, *Thomas Jefferson: Author of America*. This was, in hindsight, sort of a strange period in the ideological amblings of Hitch, who at the time was a staunch defender of Operation Iraqi Freedom, which I believe he viewed as a worthwhile war of intervention that sought to eliminate a dictator who had done some pretty bad things, not all that long ago. This stance was certainly a departure from his previous positions, sandwiched

8

between one book which took Henry Kissinger to task for his foreign policy aggressions, and what would become his writing legacy later in life, battling against the dangers of violent religious extremism. All withstanding, Hitchens was everything his fans and critics claim him to be that night: brilliant, stilted, and sarcastic, yes; but also incredibly passionate, endearingly honest, and always morally-guided and justice-seeking. My biggest regret from that night is not standing in that long line after the lecture to meet him. That misgiving aside, it was a powerful performance for me to witness at an impressionable college age, and it convinced me that writing and speaking about history and politics, and trying to do so in an honest and impassioned way, might be a decent way to make a modest but rewarding living.

I went on to major in Political Science, and received B.A. and M.A. degrees in the discipline from two of the University of Illinois campuses. Along the way, I volunteered and interned my way across state and national Democratic politics, and grew increasingly frustrated with how little it felt like either Party was really doing to address a lot of serious political issues.

That leads us into today: a turbulent US foreign policy abroad, widespread domestic and international warrantless eavesdropping by the NSA, the threat of global warming becoming increasingly serious by the day, and exploding income inequality are all just a few starting points of a grand national debate that will determine our fate as a nation in the coming years. Other "rules of the game" type issues, such as the negative effects that big money has played in campaign and legislative politics, have become unsavory to even discuss, thanks mostly to the repetitive arguments and clichéd dialogue used by those who address it. But this has happened partially because the answer is so straightforward, and the solution seemingly so unreachable. Americans who choose to zone out on politics and current affairs, preferring to embrace the many incredible diversions that are available to us today, can hardly be blamed for losing interest in a system that doesn't seem to be all that interested in them, their lives, or their personal well-being.

But here lies our biggest problem, as well. The more alienated we feel, and the more apathetic we become, also turns into the moment when we start to give in, and commit that grave sin of giving the power we hold away to those who already possess too much of it. The less we believe in American democracy, and our ability to use politics as a means to improve our nation, and gain a more responsive government, the less likely we are to actually improve a system that people from all sides of the aisle agree needs some "help," to put it mildly. The now-late, forever great Robin Williams once said, "No matter what people tell you, words and ideas can change the world." In an increasingly cynical political world, I think we'd do well to remember that anything is possible, if we want it badly enough.

I offer this "guide" as a means to contribute to ongoing discussions that I believe we as citizens can affect positively. And of course, part of the fun of the game is the "black art" of political science, trying to look into the national crystal ball of elections, and making winner/loser predictions, usually based off of hastily-amassed (but valuable) survey data. I'll look at the big races in each state, and offer some hopefully useful analysis, along with a few things for voters to consider, before heading into the polling booth.

Chapter 1

State of the Nation? Cranky, mostly.

Americans, historically, don't really like politics or politicians. Washington Post columnist E.J. Dionne covered this probably the best of anybody in his book *Why Americans Hate Politics*. I would agree with his assessment that the parties are largely offering two lines of ideology that people simply don't believe can be acted upon. But I also think the information environment has changed in a way that has allowed politics, and especially campaigns, to become more of an annoyance than anything else, to a lot of people.

I myself have mixed feelings about this situation; I get as annoyed as anyone, but I also admit to being guilty of catching the election bug every two years when autumn rolls around. There's something active and exciting about selecting a new group of people who are charged with representing your interests. Whether or not those elected actually do that is another discussion entirely, but certainly an important factor that people weigh in deciding whether or not to head to the polls.

These are also important, complex times, in an era when both our leaders and the American public at large are struggling to grasp our redefined role in a globalized economic world. Engaged citizens and activists have taken acute notice at how difficult it seems to change our current system, which seems to favor the country's wealthy and well-connected so heavily.

On that cheery note, let's have a look at some numbers and see how everyone's feeling!

The most recent Gallup poll (at this point taken 9/25 - 9/27/2014), shows that 42% approve of Barack Obama's handling of the country, versus 53% who disapprove. That's not great, but wait till you see Congress's numbers.

In an Economist/YouGov poll taken 9/20 - 9/22/2014, a pitiful 9% approve of the job Congress is doing, while 74% disapprove. In a word, yow-zah. The same poll found that 30% believe the US is on the right track, while 62% think we're on the wrong one.

Obamacare, or if you get all uppity about the name, The Affordable Care Act, the signature legislative accomplishment of the Obama Administration, comes in at "meh," in a CBS News/NY Times poll conducted 9/12 - 9/15/2014, with 41% approving of it, and 51% disapproving. This is strikingly close to the President's job approval ratings. Coincidence, anyone? Yeah, pretty unlikely...

The Pew Research Center asked for Party ID in a poll that ran from 9/2 – 9/9/2014, and found 33% of respondents declared to be Democrats, 24% considered themselves Republicans, and a whopping 38% were too disgusted to refer to themselves as either such vulgar term. I mean, why beat yourself up, right?

And perhaps our saddest number, Gallup asked in a poll that ran from 9/4 - 9/7/2014, "How satisfied are you currently?" 1,017 Americans responded that only 23% are satisfied, while a pouting 76% responded that things are just kind of dissatisfying right now.

Well I say hey America, cheer up a little bit! In our last "How's it going?" metric, the Labor Department's jobs report, unemployment numbers are generally down from where they were, at 6.1% for August 2014. The peak during the last 15 years was 10.0% in October 2009, but we've steadily shed about 1 percentage point per year since then, after being at 7.8% when Barack Obama assumed office in 2009. Now, these jobs may not actually pay enough to live off of, but it's better than sitting around at home taking naps all day, right? Though, let's admit it, naps would probably have the highest poll rating of all.

Okay, I've put you through enough of those mystifying and mostly depressing poll numbers. Let's talk about some elections...

Chapter 2

Previous Elections, and What They Mean for 2014

Recent elections tell different stories, depending on which year they were held, of course. The 2012 Presidential election was a reasonably good year for Democrats; especially when compared with 2010. President Obama won re-election without much drama, but there wasn't a big change in terms of Congressional seats. Democrats picked up 8 seats in the House, taking their total up to 201, from 193. That net loss of 8 seats took Republicans from 242 to 234, but still left them with a sizable majority; with 435 total seats, a count of 218 is needed to be the party in power.

Every two years, 33 of the US Senate seats go up for election, and this yielded a 2-seat gain for Democrats, taking their total to 53; 2 Independents also caucus with Democrats, Angus King of Maine and Bernie Sanders of Vermont. Effectively, that left 45 Republicans in the Senate, but due to several upcoming retirements by Democratic Senators in swing states, it's the real battleground for 2014. The House is seen as a sure Republican hold, so basically if Republicans pick up 6 Senate seats or more, they'll be able to try to ruin Barack Obama's life even more often than they have from 2010 to 2014, with just their House majority.

2012 gives us a few clues of what to expect, but without anyone running for President this year, it makes a lot more sense to examine a few of the previous midterm elections. I think 2010, 2006, and 1998 become the ones worth looking into the most, due to current electoral circumstances.

2010 was a veritable Republican hurricane: after a divisive fight to pass healthcare reform legislation, the immigration debate in Arizona raising tempers, and unemployment still high after a massive bail-out of Wall Street and American car manufacturers, Republicans capitalized on uncertainty about the direction of the

Obama Administration's goals, and used fiery Tea Party rhetoric to ignite their base and sway undecided voters. This was the 1994 Republican Revolution repeated 16 years later. An astonishing 63 House seats were picked up by the Republican Party; the largest transfer of House membership since 1948. This took their seat count up to 242 from 179; Democrats dropped from 257 seats to 193. The Senate wasn't as bad for Democrats, but it wasn't great either; a net loss of 6 shrunk their membership to 51 seats, and took Republicans up to 47. Democrats lost their supermajority in the Senate, totally lost the House, and life became much harder for Barack Obama, only two years into a historic Presidency that promised so much.

A lot of analysts look to 2010 as a sign of things to come for Democrats in 2014, and while I don't think that's incorrect, the two years I want to focus on are 2006, the final midterm before the end of George W. Bush's Presidency, and 1998, the final one before Bill Clinton exited office in 2000. These are the true equivalents of 2014; after 6 years in power, even popular Presidents have faded often into becoming "just another one of those guys…" This is especially dangerous for Democrats right now; Obama has become toxic in a lot of swing states, and it's hard to run with him when campaigning. A lot of nervous incumbents have decided to not mention him unless it really needs to be done. But with Congressional approval only at 9%, clearly America is frustrated with House Republicans and a Congress that just won't pass anything, either. I don't think this is another 2010 because GOP animosity has largely registered as existing with a lot of voters, which hadn't happened in 2010. For a little more guidance, let's look at 2006.

2006 has all the makings of 2014, in some ways. People had grown tired of Bush, impatient with the War in Iraq, and while the economy seemed stable, it wasn't knocking it out of the park either. That, uhh, one BIG thing hadn't happened yet (you know, the global financial crisis). Immigration was heating up as an issue, and people were starting to get ADHD about the not-that-far-off 2008 Presidential race. Essentially, this second midterm is the second-to-last date of a relationship that's been dragging your will to live out slowly for a while now; you still need an out, but the light at the end of the tunnel is becoming visible. Democrats, the opposition party at this point, ended up gaining 6 Senate seats, 31 House seats, and won 6 additional Governorships. To borrow the heartache of Jimmy Carter and Pat Caddell, malaise had fully settled in regarding the Bush White House, and people wanted to go a different direction.

This put Democrats into the House majority, and made Nancy Pelosi the first female Speaker of the House; it gave Democrats 49 Senate seats, and things officially started to lean leftward after being so comfortable for Republicans for 6 years. I think the net gain of 6 Senate seats for the opposition party (in our 2014 case, it's Republicans) is close to what everyone expects them to pick up this year. I think it could be as few as 4, but that depends on how the races go.

However, the big difference this year compared to eight years ago is how little activity we'll likely see in the US House; part of this is the national mood going against President Obama and his Party, but the other is the fact that redrawn districts benefitting Republicans from 2010 are less likely to change hands with a big Republican House majority anyway. That isn't to say the American public is pleased about their obstructionism, but with an equally strong anti-Obama headwind blowing in, districts that have been drawn to benefit Republicans are for the most part going to just stay Republican, though maybe by lesser margins than they did in 2010. Let's see if our final year has anything to tell us.

1998 was certainly a unique year. Bill Clinton was on the rebound after winning a resounding re-election in 1996, and with the economy picking up, he had relatively high approval numbers, despite his...morality issue, which broke out and reared its ugly head again in 1998, this time involving "that woman," White House Intern Monica Lewinsky. Neither party made gains in the Senate, as Republicans won Senate seats from Illinois, Kentucky, and Ohio, while Democrats won an equal number of seats in New York, North Carolina, and Indiana. And strangely enough, Democrats actually picked up 5 House seats.

This was the first time since 1934 that the non-presidential party failed to gain Congressional seats in a midterm, and remarkably, was the first time since 1822 that the non-presidential party didn't gain any seats in the midterm election of a president's second term. It's pretty widely believed that Republicans pushing for Clinton's impeachment, which a majority of voters were opposed to, according to polling, led to a backlash in what should have been a big Republican year. Okay, we'll have to call this one an outlier, because you can't really replicate those circumstances even if you tried, and that's probably a good thing.

So, where does this leave us? I would say this year looks much more like the conventional "six year itch," a term political scientists use to describe the second midterm of an 8-year Presidency. My feeling is that it looks the most like 2006, in terms of national mood and feeling, with Republicans picking up Senate seats and likely adding a few to an already big House majority. Of course, the specifics of those races matter, so let's dig in and see where things might be heading.

Chapter 3

2014 State-by-State Election Analysis (Alphabetical)

[Note: (R) denotes Republican, (D) denotes Democrat, (I) denotes Independent, (L) denotes Libertarian (G) denotes Green; all third-party candidates who are believed to affect a race will be included in listed candidates; Incumbents are denoted by an asterisk after their Party (*)]

Alabama

Governor: Robert Bentley (R)* vs. Parker Griffith (D)

Senate: Jeff Sessions (R)* vs. Nobody!?

Featured House Race: Alabama 1 – Bradley Byrne (R)* vs. Burton LeFlore (D)

Analysis

Jesus, we have to start with Alabama? Well, the alphabet can be cruel, but I guess we have no choice but to begin. Not much reason to expect any surprises in 2014 from "The Yellowhammer State," (an archaic reference to a unit of Alabama soldiers from the Civil War, go figure).

Governor's race: Bentley is seeking his second term, this year against former-Democratic US Representative Parker Griffith, and enjoys a 20+ point lead in relevant polls. Enjoying a high favorability rating as well, Governor Bentley looks like the hands-down favorite to get re-hired in deep-red Alabama.

Predicted Winner: Robert Bentley (R)

Senate race: Well, not much to analyze on this one. Incumbent Republican Jeff Sessions is running unopposed in his bid for a fourth term. If you needed any proof of how much of a stranglehold Republicans have on Alabama, this removes any doubt whatsoever. This is the first time in Alabama's history the Democratic Party hasn't fielded a candidate for a US Senate race. Come on Democrats, you have to run *somebody* for a 6-year job!

Predicted Winner: I'm a risk taker, so I'll go with Jeff Sessions (R)...

Featured House race: Bradley Byrne (R) is a recent addition to the US House, winning a special election in December of 2013 to replace outgoing Representative Jo Bonner (R), who resigned the seat to accept an administrative position at the University of Alabama. He will face off against the opponent he defeated in the general election for this seat, Democrat Burton LeFlore. An attorney and son of the prominent civil rights activist John LeFlore, he failed to capture 30% of the vote in 2013.

Predicted winner: Bradley Byrne (R) looks like the obvious pick to retain his seat; he enjoys relatively high name recognition from his gubernatorial run against Bentley in 2010, a big advantage in cash-on-hand, and strong support within the district.

Don't miss: Former House Financial Services Committee Chairman Spencer Bachus (R) is retiring from the AL-6 seat after a 20 year career; the seat is expected to stay Republican.

Alaska

Governor: Sean Parnell (R)* vs. Bill Walker (I); Byron Mallott (D) dropped off the ballot

Senate: Mark Begich (D)* vs. Dan Sullivan (R)

Featured House Race: Alaska At-Large – Don Young (R)* vs. Forrest Dunbar (D) vs. Jim Mcdermott (L)

Analysis

Alaska, or "The Last Frontier," in a nod to its lightly settled regions, was a lot more fun when it involved Sarah Palin's crazy ass. Although, between the launch of the Sarah Palin Channel and recent news that the Palin clan was involved in an alcohol-fueled brawl at a "snow machine" party in Anchorage, Palin-lovers can still get their fix without the rest of the country suffering.

Governor's race: Parnell is running for his second term as Palin's successor. Democrat Byron Mallott was dropped from the ballot by Alaska Democrats after the primary, who subsequently threw their support behind Independent Bill Walker, former Mayor of Valdez. This change has thrown the race into toss-up mode, making Parnell's sure bet re-election into a real fight.

Predicted winner: A tough call, but I think Bill Walker (I) pulls it out; his popularity with Independents and moderates, paired with Democratic Party support, should be enough to win this.

Senate race: Mark Begich (D) is a man who finds himself in the middle of national Republican crosshairs. He pulled off a pretty big upset in 2008 over longtime Senate heavyweight Ted "The Internet is a series of tubes" Stevens, who during the election was suffering through a federal corruption trial, which eventually found him to be guilty. Begich, helped along by that and a big turnout for the landmark election of Barack Obama in 2008, was able to flip a reliably-red seat in a year that contributed to Senate Democrats gaining a supermajority of seats until 2010.

But matters are much more difficult this time around, and we've seen the Begich campaign's desperation in full force. With the release of a Willie Horton-style ad, directed at opponent Dan Sullivan, the former Attorney General of Alaska, the Begich people lost some important credibility. The ad had to be pulled due to inaccuracy of the claim that Sullivan was indirectly responsible for putting a prisoner on probation who committed a double murder and sex crime; it is the kind of ad that, if accurate, has the potency to destroy an opponent in one fell swoop, in the same manner that the Horton ad dashed Michael Dukakis's chances in 1988. However, if the charges don't line up correctly, it breaks a cardinal rule of campaign advertising: if you go dirty, it has to be accurate; otherwise you risk your reputation, and become the mud-slinging politician that voters love to vote against. Unfortunately for Begich and company, Sullivan took office as Attorney General after the probation decision for Jerry Active had been reached, and had little-to-no ability to reverse that. Long story short, Begich needed to run a flawless campaign to hold this seat, and that's already not possible. He could still win this, but it would be a surprise to a lot of people, including me.

Predicted winner: Dan Sullivan (R), in a return to Alaskan predictability for Stevens' former seat

Featured House race: Don Young (R) is expected to hold onto the seat he has occupied since 1973, with very little drama. He became Alaska's House Member At-Large by winning an election to fill the office after the tragic plane crash and ensuing disappearance of then-officeholder and Democrat Nick Begich, Mark's father.

Arizona

Governor: Fred DuVal (D) vs. Doug Ducey (R); Jan Brewer is term-limited out of office

Senate: No 2014 race; John McCain (R) is eligible for re-election in 2016

Featured House Race: Arizona 2 – Ron Barber (D)* vs. Martha McSally (R)

Analysis

Not surprisingly, things have turned hot in "The Grand Canyon State" during Governor Jan Brewer's tenure. A résumé that includes refusing to shake Obama's hand on the tarmac during a Presidential visit, support of the nation's most controversial immigration law in SB 1070, and a disappointingly muted response to gun control requests after the tragic shooting of US Representative Gabrielle Giffords, Brewer's legacy is up in the air, to put it mildly.

Governor's race: This race is surprisingly tight for what seemed to be an increasingly-Republican Arizona. Brewer, who's generated a lot of national attention for her views on immigration policy and border enforcement, is term-limited out of office after only assuming the job in 2009, following the departure of Democrat Janet Napolitano to serve in the Obama administration. Arizona law dictates that no Governor serve more than two consecutive terms in office, even if they are abbreviated. After considering a legal challenge, Brewer decided not to pursue the action.

The resulting race pits Republican State Treasurer Doug Ducey against Democrat Fred DuVal, the Former President of the Arizona Board of Regents. The debates will be key in this race, along with campaign messaging, with things so close. Napolitano left Arizona with a high favorability rating to become the Secretary of Homeland Security, and rumors are that the moderate base in Arizona has grown increasingly discontent with some of the hardline policies pursued by Brewer. That said, DuVal will have to make a strong showing to beat Ducey, in a state that seems more than comfortable with its two Republican Senators, John McCain and Jeff Flake.

Predicted winner: A lot will unfold in this toss-up before Election Day, but DuVal is a strong candidate in a state that seems ready for a change. A close one, but I'm going with Fred Duval (D).

John McCain, who would be 80 in 2016, has hinted at possibly retiring at the end of his current term, but he'd obviously be a lock to win if he didn't.

Featured House race: Barber is a former staffer for Gabrielle Giffords, who assumed her term for her after she had to resign for health reasons in 2011. He won a narrow race as a moderate Democrat for the seat in 2012, and matches up another time against Republican Martha McSally, the first female fighter pilot in US history. This is viewed as one of the ten toughest seats to defend in 2014, and without the Presidential election bump Barber received in 2012, it looks like a tough hold for Democrats.

Predicted winner: Martha McSally (R)

Arkansas

Governor: Asa Hutchinson (R) vs. Mike Ross (D); Mike Beebe (D) is term-limited out of office

Senate: Mark Pryor (D)* vs. Tom Cotton (R)

Featured House Race: Arkansas 2 – French Hill (R) vs. Patrick Henry Hays (D)

Analysis

Arkansas, or "The Natural State" for its "natural beauty, clear lakes and streams and abundance of natural wildlife" has been trending red since the Blanche Lincoln blowout of 2010, and while Democratic Governor Mike Beebe departs in high regard due to term limits, this looks like a hard year for Arkansas Democrats.

Governor's race: Former US Representative and business consultant Asa Hutchinson holds a steady lead over highly-touted Democratic recruit Mike Ross. Hutchinson lost to the popular Beebe in 2006, but in some ways seems like the natural successor for the job after raising his name recognition. Ross was a 12-year member of the US House before resigning his post to accept a position in the private sector. Tom Cotton, the Republican nominee for Senate this year, took his Congressional seat in 2012. Oh, what a tangled web we weave.

Predicted winner: Hutchinson's polling has looked good against Ross since the primary, and I don't see any big surprises in the future. I'm going with Asa Hutchinson (R).

Senate race: And here we are. One of the most hotly-contested Senate races of the term, Republican whiz kid and freshman House member Tom Cotton seeks to flip Democrat Mark Pryor out of a Senate seat he's kept warm for twelve years. Pryor, a centrist Democrat, isn't facing the heat that Lincoln did in 2010 from Arkansas voters, but he does have to contend with a boatload of outside Republican money, and Cotton himself, whose profile as a farmer, Harvard Law graduate, and Iraq War veteran has both Tea Party and establishment appeal.

That said, Democrats are trying equally hard to protect this seat, and Pryor has made a name for himself as a steady moderate hand in the Senate, for a state that doesn't traditionally vote as Republican as those in the Deep South. Though he does sort of come off as a bookish, glassesed liberal, Pryor addressed that image issue in an ad describing the Bible, or Good Book, as "his moral compass." Pryor was a "yea" vote on the Affordable Care Act, which could be a liability for a lot of Senators this year, and Cotton is going to great pains to make sure that association sticks. Cotton recently took some criticism from Democrats for running an ad describing the Farm Bill he voted against as a bill that Obama loaded down with food stamp legislation, which has demonstrated to be pretty patently not true by several fact checkers. This is a big deal for the same reason the Begich ad was; as dirty as political ads can be, they have to be true. It may result in a backlash for Cotton.

Predicted Winner: This one's really up for grabs; Cotton has had a 3-to-5 point lead in most polls, though Pryor's established name gives him some credibility. I think Cotton's rising-star profile wins it for him though. Tom Cotton (R) in a close one.

Featured House Race: This is an interesting one because AR-2 is so unpredictable. Composed of Little Rock and its suburbs, it's been sort of a wild card in terms of electoral history. Sending both somewhat liberal and dedicated conservatives to Congress, it has trended more red than blue recently. Hill, a former White House Republican aide, has a slight polling advantage over Hays, a former North Little Rock Mayor.

Predicted Winner: French Hill (R)

Don't miss: Bill Clinton has been an active campaigner for both big-race Arkansas Democrats, and it could be enough help to put Pryor over the top. He may not recognize the state that made his political career as much these days, though.

California

Governor: Jerry Brown (D)* vs. Neel Kashkari (R)

Senate: No 2014 race; Barbara Boxer (D) is eligible for re-election in 2016

Featured House Race: California 36 – Raul Ruiz (D)* vs. Brian Nestande (R)

Analysis

California, or "The Golden State," can trace its modern development back to the discovery of gold in 1848, and the name also references the fields of golden poppies that can be seen each spring throughout the state.

Governor's race: The state has enjoyed a big comeback in recent years, and California political mainstay Governor Jerry Brown (D) has received a lot of credit for it. In a time when most politicians are reviled somewhere in-between an ankle sprain and the 24-hour flu, Brown has seen his favorability soar above 55% for most of his latest (third) non-consecutive term, and even hit 60% a few times. Along with presiding during the state's economic turnaround, he put a cap on previously-skyrocketing state university tuition prices, and has led effectively on issues important to the state, ranging from immigration and early childhood education, to the ravenous wildfire and drought management.

The latter has resulted in his elevation to the forefront of concerned officials who are having to deal with real-world consequences from global warming. In what was originally viewed as a feeble attempt to take his old job back by Republicans and probably a bigger-than-they'd-admit-to group of Democrats in 2010, Brown is strongly favored to cruise to victory over former Bush Treasury official and engineer-turned-investment banker, Neel Kashkari (R).

Kashkari represents a switch though, and it could be an important one for Republicans who seek to compete in dark-blue states like California. Young, Indian-American, and socially moderate, Kashkari was the logical and serious pick over fellow Republican primary contender and "Send 'em back" wahoo Assemblyman Tim Donnelly. Donnelly's big claim to relevance was being hyperactively into "protecting our border," which led him to found the xenophobic California chapter of the armed militia-styled Minutemen group. His big campaign moment nationally came when he produced an ad featuring a message mentioning his "smokin' hot" wife Rowena, who is of Filipino descent, which in theory makes him seem less bigoted, but the message itself was delivered by him and oddly translated into Spanish by a Hispanic woman who was not his wife, in an obvious pander to Latino voters. Either way, the Donnelly-Kashkari divide in

Republican politics is the now-classic Tea Party versus establishment big-business Republican battle that has driven establishment-type Republicans insane since 2010, while at the same time driving their party legion numbers upward. It's worth pointing out that Kashkari very possibly got through in this race because it was an open primary: California voters sent the top two overall vote-getters into the general election, chosen from a field of nearly 10 names on the ballot. Play it out in a closed-Party primary, and there's a fair chance that the motivated hard-line Republicans turn out and send Donnelly to get destroyed by Brown, rather than the more moderate Kashkari.

Kashkari, the receptor of Karl Rove's blessing in this race (if a creature like Rove is allowed to issue such things as "blessings"), has gained some national exposure as a serious candidate for an office that may translate into valuable credibility and recognition down the line for him in a future race. George Will lauded him as the Party's "Barry Goldwater 2.0," in a salute to the reality that if Republicans are going to compete seriously in a place like California, it has to be in a return to a moderate Republican/Libertarian-styled candidate. Kashkari has performed reasonably as expected, not doing anything that may risk humiliation, thereby creating any unneeded problems with more potentially-winnable races down the line.

He promotes "Jobs and education: that's it," as his simple and effectively-direct campaign platform. He did do a little bit of backbiting though, directed at former Governor Arnold Schwarzenegger, accusing the man who played Terminator of being too afraid to take the big necessary risks and deliver the leadership that a middling California economy required during his tenure. It's the kind of backbiting you expect from passive-aggressive Democrats behind closed doors, so it was different to hear such criticism relayed directly to the press at a fellow Republican, but I think it's really more of a signal of exasperation at how strong Jerry Brown is right now. Kashkari is an interesting candidate, who gained Republican chops by being one of the big guns who oversaw the disbursal of the Bush-end of the bailout funds in 2008. His direct and at times intense manner of speech can I think both be a liability and an asset; it may play better out East, but at the very least it communicates sincerity, and a drive to work hard in whatever position the people of California may put him in.

He should also be commended for what seems like a genuine concern with poverty: he took the temporarily-homeless challenge like a few other candidates have this election season. Sure, it's a stunt, but for a former investment banker, the gesture means more than it would from a candidate from a different background. I should also admit that I'm a little bit of a homer, and have followed him closely because he received his engineering degrees at the University of Illinois, and I'm always looking for an opportunity to root for a fellow Illinois alumnus.

Predicted Winner: Democrat Jerry "Moonbeam" Brown, (thanks Mike Royko), secures his record fourth term as Governor overall, in what's become one of the great political comeback stories in a while, though I'd expect him to reassure us he never really left (and maybe he didn't, serving as California Attorney General, Secretary of State, and Mayor of Oakland in-between Governorships).

As mentioned, there is no California US Senate race this year, but it's pretty widely-acknowledged that a changing of the guard is on its way soon. Boxer is rumored to be mulling retirement over rather than run for a fifth term, which may open her seat in 2016. Former Speaker and current House Minority Leader Nancy Pelosi is 74, with retirement questions hanging around her amidst long-time allies Henry Waxman and George Miller departing from their seats this year. And 2018 looks even more hectic, with Governor

Jerry Brown term-limited out of office, and Dianne Feinstein turning 85 that June in her re-election year as well.

So, it looks more and more likely that young rising stars from the Democratic Party of California will have an opportunity to shine in the national spotlight soon. Current California Attorney General Kamala Harris, and former San Francisco Mayor-turned-Lieutenant Governor Gavin Newsom, seem like the obvious favorites to succeed their party elder (literally) predecessors, and the aforementioned Kashkari will have his own choice of which seat to pursue, one might think, as the de facto prominent Republican candidate. Representative Kevin McCarthy of Bakersfield has found his way into Majority Leader of the US House Republicans, taking over Eric Cantor's old job in June, which while it undoubtedly raises his profile nationally, may be a rather dubious kiss of death in a statewide California race. Regardless of how it unfolds, it should be hectic, expensive, and a lot of fun to watch.

Featured House race: Back to this year, CA-36 looks like a good race. Superhuman and freshman Congressman Raul Ruiz looks to recapture his seat in a tough district for Democrats. Ruiz, who holds an MD, MPH, and MPP from Harvard, and was previously employed as an emergency room physician, upset a heavily-favored but redistricted Mary Bono Mack (R) in 2012. Ruiz faces political consultant-turned-politician Brian Nestande, currently the Assemblyman for the 42nd Palm Springs district. It's considered a toss-up and one of the toughest seats to hold nationally, so it may very well flip without the Obama bump that helped Ruiz two years ago. But Ruiz is a special candidate, so I like him to repeat again in a tough district.

Predicted Winner: Raul Ruiz (D)

Colorado

Governor: John Hickenlooper (D)* vs. Bob Beauprez (R)

Senate: Mark Udall (D)* vs. Cory Gardner (R)

Featured House Race: Colorado 6 – Mike Coffman (R)* vs. Andrew Romanoff (D)

Analysis

"The Centennial State," admitted to our fine union in 1876, has been more politically unpredictable than imagined lately. Both marquis races are toss-ups right now, and could remain that way until Election Day.

Governor's race: Hickenlooper, or as I like to call him, "Governor Ganja," is in a tight one for re-election against Republican hopeful and former US Congressman Bob Beauprez. Polling has been back and forth on this one, but I have a feeling he'll benefit from a decent turnout for Senator Mark Udall on the same ballot. All weed jokes aside, one has to wonder if legalizing marijuana statewide has an electoral effect, based on the new population potentially drawn to the state.

Of course, the question becomes how motivated are those folks to register to vote in a new state, and vote on Election Day? It could be enough to make a difference, and at this point Hickenlooper will take all the help he can get, after Colorado Democrats suffered the loss of two recalled Democratic state senators in 2013, and had to swallow the resignation of a third, as well. Things certainly seem to be trending Republican in a state that experienced a GOP collapse in 2010, which cleared the way for Hickenlooper in the first place.

Predicted winner: It's close, but I think Bob Beauprez (R), who ran for the job in 2006, pulls it out; Hickenlooper and statehouse

Democrats both have registered some trust problems in recent polling, and it's hard to overcome that in a close race.

Senate race: Mark Udall (D) won in 2008 in the political windfall that gave the Democrats their big Senate majority thanks in part to Barack Obama's long coattails. But Udall also comes from a politically prominent family in the West, which never hurts to raise a candidate's profile. What really makes this race tough for him is the quality of his challenger, Republican rising star and US Representative Cory Gardner. Udall is reasonably well-respected though, and while polling is back-and-forth, he holds a big enough incumbent advantage that a Gardner win would be a definite upset. Udall has also been a leading figure, along with Senator Ron Wyden, in trying to rein in the NSA surveillance programs. So I think he's doing important work, which never hurts when it comes to arguing for a reappointment.

Predicted Winner: Mark Udall (D) holds on in a close one.

Featured House race: CO-6 is destined to be a good one for a while; it leans slightly Democratic, but Mike Coffman (R) is a good candidate who won the seat in a tough 2012. Democrats put a lot of early money behind challenger and former Speaker of the Colorado House Andrew Romanoff, but my feeling is that if this didn't go Democrat in 2012, it's very unlikely to in 2014.

Predicted winner: Mike Coffman (R)

Connecticut

Governor: Dannel Malloy (D)* vs. Tom Foley (R)

Senate: No race; Richard Blumenthal (D) is eligible for re-election in 2016

Featured House Race: Connecticut 5 – Elizabeth Esty (D)* vs. Mark Greenberg (R)

Analysis

"The Constitution State," or if we're being honest here, "Land Full of Wealthy White People," claims to have been responsible for producing the first constitution of the United States in 1763. Let's just give them the benefit of the doubt and go along with it.

Governor's race: Rich guy and former Ambassador to Ireland under George W. Bush, Republican Tom Foley, challenges Malloy for the job again, a rematch from 2010. Malloy, who has had a controversial four years, has struggled to gain much traction in this race. He is viewed as seriously endangered in this contest, especially after barely defeating Foley in 2010. Foley has received a good number of national Republicans to stump for him this time around, including NJ Governor Chris Christie.

Predicted winner: Tom Foley (R); I think Republicans just want this one more.

While there is no Senate race this year, I think we can all be grateful for Joe Lieberman's retirement.

Featured House race: Mark Greenberg (R) hopes his third time's the charm running in this district, as he seeks to unseat former attorney and one-term Congresswoman Elizabeth Esty. Democrats have poured some money into defending this one, which is Senator Chris Murphy's old seat. The polls point to Esty hanging on, and I think she does.

Predicted winner: Elizabeth Esty (D)

DC

At-Large – Eleanor Holmes Norton (D) has served as a "non-voting member" of the U.S. House of Representatives since 1990, with the title of Delegate from the District of Columbia. This is slightly misleading, because while she cannot vote on final bills that reach the reach the House floor, her vote does count in the committees she serves on. She is running for re-election in 2014, and will have no issues winning a decisive victory.

I wanted to take the opportunity to say a few things about DC, even though obviously there are no gubernatorial or Senate elections, and the one House election is basically decided. I've lived briefly in DC twice; the first time as an intern on Capitol Hill in 2006. I laughed at the "Taxation without Representation" slogan on the license plates, thinking "Are these people serious? It's 230 years after the Revolutionary War and this is what they put on their plates?" But after doing a little more research on the battle for DC statehood, I started to realize what a strange—and yes, unfair, arrangement the city of Washington, DC is for a lot of the people who live there.

DC's yearly budget is appropriated from federal funds that are often used in a type of weird partisan kickball, and there are no voting federal representatives to voice opposition or support for any measures. DC itself has a population of over 630,000 now, which makes it bigger than Wyoming and Vermont; both respectively have three voting members of Congress each. Size aside, it's difficult to say what exactly is holding back the progress from DC being granted statehood. It may be because we haven't done that since 1959, with Alaska and Hawaii making a nice, round, even 50 states. It may be because what are we going to do, put an extra star on the flag? Where is that going to go without looking stupid?

I don't know, but it's time to finally give the poor saps a break. Preventing the people who are the biggest and most obsessed partisan lunatics from having a real voting representation in Congress seems like a cruel (if not funny) joke, much less everyone else who has to put up with them. And it certainly adds to the weird black hole/Bermuda Triangle effect of living and working in DC...both the hub of Western democracy, and the city without a state or a Senator.

Delaware

Governor: No race; Jack Markell (D) is up in 2016

Senate: Chris Coons (D)* vs. Kevin Wade (R) vs. Andrew Groff (G)

Featured House Race: Delaware At-Large – John Carney (D)* vs. Rose Izzo (R) vs. Scott Gesty (L) vs. Bernard August (G)

Analysis

"The First State" became the first of the 13 original states to ratify the U.S. Constitution on December 7, 1787. It also has the somewhat dubious distinction of being a tax shelter for American banks and corporations who have remained loyal enough to not totally move operations offshore. Jack Markell (D) won his 2012 bid by over 40% for Governor, causing some speculation that he might seek the national spotlight in 2016. He hasn't committed to anything beyond supporting Vice President Joe Biden for President, if he should choose to run.

Senate: Chris Coons (D), perhaps the Senator with the most unfortunate last name, has a double digit lead over Republican challenger Kevin Wade. Don't take him lightly though, Coons has some serious policy credentials and an interesting background, graduating from Yale Divinity School. He won the special election for Joe Biden's seat in 2010, and looks to be there for a long time.

Predicted winner: Chris Coons (D)

Featured House race: Democrat John Carney has served as Delaware's At-Large Congressman since 2011. He was the 24th Lieutenant Governor of Delaware from 2001 to 2009, and looks like a sure-thing to hold his seat against a handful of candidates, including Republican and proud housewife Rose Izzo.

Predicted winner: John Carney (D)

Don't miss: Adorable Tea Party lunatic Christine O'Donnell declined to run for this Senate seat again, after losing by 17% in 2010 to Coons.

Florida

Governor: Rick Scott (R)* vs. Charlie Crist (D)

Senate: No race; Marco Rubio (R) is up in 2016

Featured House Race: Florida 18 – Patrick Murphy (D)* vs. Carl Domino (R)

"The Sunshine State" has been working on building up a strange reputation over the past few years, thanks to bath salts being consumed, George Zimmerman, and the tragic breakup of America's favorite sports team, the Miami Heat. Their politics are about as hectic as the aforementioned.

Governor's race: Incumbent Rick Scott (R) gets some cool points for looking like Hitman, as in the Agent 47, video game variety. Outside of that, he's had some problems over the past four years. He is however not going lightly, and if 2010 showed us anything, he's capable of both raising and spending a ton of his own venture capitalist money to win a close race.

Crist has done the full chameleon over the past four years, changing from Republican red to Democrat blue. Before leaving the Governor's office as a Republican in 2011, he ran for retiring Senator Mel Martinez's seat in 2010, but lost the Republican primary to then-Tea Party darling Marco Rubio. Crist decided to run as an Independent in that race, but only captured 30% of the vote, with not-so-thrilled Democrat Kendrick Meeks taking 20%. With Scott in the Governor's mansion as a Republican, Crist found himself endorsing Barack Obama in 2012 for re-election. The move wasn't a big leap really, with Crist being a moderate and reasonably active on the climate change awareness front anyway.

A clear favorite heading into the matchup against Hitman, Crist did lose some serious Florida brownie points after the *Tampa Bay Times* published a deeply-detailed profile of his political maneuvering within the state of Florida, which I was directed to by Chris Cilizza's "The Fix" political blog. To say Crist comes off as opportunistic, self-interested, and not exactly enthralled with the policymaking process is an understatement. That said, he's got a political gift for connecting with people, and he's had a long history of representing Florida in a manner that many voters approved of. If he can make the case that a vote for Charlie is one for going back to "the Florida you used to know," it's his for the taking.

Predicted winner: Even with Scott's money and big supporters behind him, it's hard to see Crist losing again. Charlie Crist (D) in a close, and ugly one.

Someone get Marco Rubio a drink, he's awfully parched. Florida's a hot, humid, sweaty place.

Featured House race: The unfortunately-opinionated Allen West's old seat is up for grabs after youthful accountant Pat Murphy (D) upset him in 2012. Former member of the Florida House Carl Domino is seeking to take the seat back for Republicans. Murphy has done what he can to establish himself as a bipartisan, moderate fit in Congress for the district, but I think it's a really tough hold for Democrats in a district that leans Republican anyway.

Predicted winner: Carl Domino (R)

Georgia

Governor: Nathan Deal (R)* vs. Jason Carter (D)

Senate: Michelle Nunn (D) vs. David Perdue (R); Senator Saxby Chambliss (R) is retiring

Featured House Race: Georgia 12 – John Barrow (D)* vs. Rick Allen (R)

Analysis

Georgia is known as the "Peach State" because of the growers' reputation for producing the highest quality fruit. However, the peach only became the official state fruit in 1995!

Governor's race: Republican Nathan Deal, who's gained a national reputation as highly conservative, has really struggled lately. This race is tied or trending towards Carter, depending on which poll you're looking at. Deal has to prove he's still the man for the job (with his back up against the wall, nonetheless), rather than Carter. As the grandson of President Jimmy Carter and a popular State Senator, he has a lot of political goodwill to cash in on. Georgia governorships also have a long history of being much more Democratically-inclined than one might think, so it wouldn't be a huge surprise to see this go back to Democrats.

Predicted winner: Jason Carter (D)

Senate race: This is another all-in-the-family type of affair, with Nunn being the daughter of former Senator Sam Nunn, and Perdue the cousin of former Georgia Governor Sonny Perdue. The Nunn campaign made one of the more impressive gaffes of this election cycle, when someone leaked their whole campaign plan in late July to the media. They've largely recovered because she's a good candidate, but wow, how do you explain that one to the boss? I was surprised to see Nunn hold onto a lead for as long as she had, and while it's still a close race, Perdue is picking up steam at a good time. It's just hard to see both of these Georgia seats going Democrat in 2014, too.

Predicted winner: David Perdue (R)

Barrow, a Harvard Law graduate, is sort of a survivor. He upset Rep. Max Burns in 2004, and has been winning elections he wasn't supposed to ever since. The district keeps getting more Republican, and he wins anyway. He's viewed as highly vulnerable this year, but it's on businessman Rick Allen to take him down, and I won't believe it till I see it.

Predicted winner: John Barrow (D)

Hawaii

"The Aloha State," surprise.

Governor: Duke Aiona (R) vs. David Ige (D) vs. Mufi Hannemann (I)

Senate: Brian Schatz (D)* vs. Cam Cavasso (R)

Featured House Race: Hawaii 2 – Tulsi Gabbard (D)* vs. Kawika Crowley (R) vs. Joe Kent (L)

Governor's race: Talk about drama. Aged-hippie and Obama friend Neil Abercrombie got primaried out of his job by David Ige this year, thanks in part to Abercrombie tapping his Lieutenant Governor Brian Schatz to fill the Senate seat vacated by dearly departed chubby girl admirer Daniel Inouye. Inouye had, on his deathbed nonetheless, made his wish be known that US Representative Colleen Hanabusa be appointed to his seat to finish out the term. Obviously, naming Schatz to the seat was risky, and it's believed that Abercrombie paid the price for pissing off the Democratic Party of Hawaii.

There's also a conspiracy theory that Ige picked up a lot of support in the primary from Republicans who voted Democrat, in order to put a more beatable candidate there; so far it looks like Ige holds the close edge over Aiona, a former Hawaiian Lieutenant Governor. Hannemann, the former Democratic Mayor of Honolulu, is making this race really interesting, pulling 10-to-15% away from Ige. This race is way closer than Democrats want it to be, regardless of how divided the party is over the Hanabusa snubbing. Welcome to the Jersey Shore, Hawaii edition.

Predicted winner: No one would be surprised if Aiona pulled this out, but I'm still going with Democrat David Ige. He will likely benefit from united Democratic Party support in the coming weeks. And, it's still Hawaii, a stronghold for Democrats.

Senate race: After surviving a predictably-nasty primary challenge from the spurned Hanabusa, and winning by less than 1%, Schatz is laughing all the way back to Washington for six more years. He currently leads former Hawaii House member Cam Cavasso by a stunning 25%. This is significant for a few reasons: if you want to see how Hannemann's presence is affecting the Governor's race, just look at polling numbers for this one. One has to wonder about Hanabusa's decision to challenge the popular Schatz rather than a flailing Abercrombie; it makes sense that she would pursue the seat that Inouye wanted her in, but there's no doubt that Abercrombie was more vulnerable, and after all, he was probably the one who most deserved her channeled anger, after being the one to make the Inouye-replacement decision. Mmmm...politics.

Predicted winner: Brian Schatz (D), with ease.

Featured House race: Gabbard (D), who's the daughter of two politically-influential Democrats, has a lot going for her; this will be an easy hold. She was the first Hindu elected to Congress, winning in 2012. She beat Crowley for this seat handily two years ago.

Predicted winner: Tulsi Gabbard (D)

Idaho

Governor: Butch Otter (R)* vs. A.J. Balukoff (D)

Senate: Jim Risch (R)* vs. Nels Mitchell (D)

Featured House Race: Idaho 1 – Raul Labrador (R)* vs. Shirley Ringo (D)

Analysis

Well, the Gem State (What, no potato reference? Come on, guys...) is pretty much in the figurative "sack" for Republicans. Ballotpedia informs us that "No Democrat has been elected to the Senate from Idaho since 1974, and a Democrat has been elected only once to the House since 1992." So...let's not waste any time creating something that just isn't there, with all respect to the Democratic challengers, who I'm sure are working their hardest.

Predicted winners: Governor Butch Otter (R) by 15%, Senator Jim Risch (R) might win his race by 30%, and Representative Raul Labrador (R) by who cares%.

Indiana

Governor: No race; Mike Pence (R) is up in 2016

Senate: No race; Dan Coats (R) is up in 2016

Featured House race: IN-2: Jackie Walorski (R)* vs. Joe Bock (D)

Analysis

After breaking for Obama in 2008, thanks mostly to heavy registration drives held by Illinoisans crossing the border, "The Hoosier State," has for the most part gone back to its predictable shade of red. The "Hoosier State" nickname came into general usage in the 1830s, when John Finley wrote a poem, "The Hoosier's Nest," for the Indianapolis Journal. It was widely copied throughout the country!

In 2012, Joe Donnelly did win a Senate seat for Democrats, thanks mostly to Tea Partier Richard Mourdock's total collapse around his statement suggesting that "a child conceived in rape was part of God's plan," after beating longtime Senator Richard Lugar in the Republican primary. Hmmm... There are no elections for Governor or Senate in 2014, so we'll take it straight to the House.

Featured House race: IN-2 is basically a Republican district that got even redder in 2010 after redistricting. Committed right-winger and former broadcast journalist Jackie Walorski looks like the favorite to hold on to this one against a Golden Domer, Notre Dame professor Joe Bock, who would be a formidable challenger in a more Democratic year.

Predicted winner: Jackie Walorski (R)

Iowa

Governor: Terry Branstad (R)* vs. Jack Hatch (D)

Senate: Bruce Braley (D) vs. Joni Ernst (R)

Featured House Race: Iowa 3 - David Young (R) vs. Staci Appel (D)

Analysis

"The Hawkeye State" moniker is a tribute to Native American Chief Black Hawk.

Governor's race: Branstad looks well on his way to becoming the official Emperor of Iowa. Popular in his first term of service from 1983 through 1999, he looks like a sure bet to cruise to a re-election victory over Iowa State Senator Jack Hatch (D). He would become the longest tenured Governor in US history if he wins and serves this next term out.

Predicted winner: Terry Branstad (R)

Senate race: Well, this is a big one for many reasons. After being there for 24 years, Iowan and US Senate mainstay Tom Harkin called it a career this year, and the race to replace him has been interesting to say the least. US Rep. Bruce Braley was the state party choice to fill a seat that looked like a pretty sure thing to stay in Democratic hands, but a campaign that's had a few too many gaffes to be called well-run has resulted in State Senator Joni Ernst (R) locking Braley in a virtual tie in polling. Ernst is sort of a Palin-type character; her introduction ad touted her resume as a "mother, solider, and conservative" who grew up on an Iowa farm "castrating hogs," which turned into a metaphor for knowing how to cut pork in Washington, DC. It's somewhere between a cute play on word, and just horrifying imagery.

Either way, there are a few reasons I think this seat stays in the hands of Democrats. It's important to remember that this is effectively still Tom Harkin's seat. His name and legacy are behind the Braley effort, and that matters. And, no matter what you might think of Iowa, it's a highly politically-aware state, thanks in part to its seat at the front of the Presidential primaries. It was also one of the earliest states to strike down its ban on same-sex marriage as unconstitutional, and has a history of embracing populist themes.

The populist streak in some ways benefits Ernst, who is charismatic in her own way, and continues to do what she can to tie Braley to Obama. But with Republican Chuck Grassley firmly seated in the other Iowa Senate seat, I think Iowans like the idea of maintaining a somewhat moderate balance of who represents them. That, ultimately, is what I think costs Ernst the race; running as a Palin-brand conservative would work in a lot of red states this year, but Iowa's much more purple than red or blue.

If Braley can avoid plugging the gaffe machine back in (stay away from those therapeutic chicken lawsuits, Bruce), he should be your winner as the common-sense moderate Democrat worthy of carrying on Harkin's populist legacy. The factor of Branstad being on the ballot needs to be considered, but I think it only helps a moderate Republican, which Ernst is not. It should be fun to watch play out.

Predicted winner: Bruce Braley (D), in a really tight one.

Featured House race: Polling puts Appel in the lead for IA-3. She was a state senator, and is competing for the open seat against the former Chief of Staff for Chuck Grassley, David Young (R). Young ended up being chosen the nominee after the primary failed to yield a winner with over 35% of the vote. Tom Latham (R) declined to run for re-election in this district, which he won in 2012, in spite of it breaking for Obama on the Presidential level. I think Appel capitalizes on the shift toward Democrats.

Predicted winner: Staci Appel (D)

Kansas

Governor: Sam Brownback (R)* vs. Paul Davis (D)

Senate: Pat Roberts (R)* vs. Greg Orman (I); Chad Taylor (D) withdrew, will not appear on the ballot

Featured House Race: Kansas 2 – Lynn Jenkins (R)* vs. Margie Wakefield (D) vs. Chris Clemmons (L)

Analysis

Kansas is nicknamed "The Sunflower State," which calls to mind the wild flowers of the plains; it's the officially-recognized state flower.

Governor's race: So Sam Brownback walks into a bar and orders a round of tax cuts…Republicans might find that setup funnier if it weren't so devastatingly true, and ripping their party apart. Brownback, who is a longtime smug face on the political scene in Kansas, tried a little neoconservative experiment with his home state, and forced massive tax cuts down Democrat and moderate-Republican throats. This wasn't well-received when it came out that education funding was going to be somewhere between $600-to-$1,000 below the national standard per pupil. Upset parents sued the state of Kansas over this budgeting, and moderate Republicans sided with them, hoping to have careers past 2014.

To make a long story short, you'd really have to fuck this one up to turn it into a good race, and Brownback has done just that. But it would be unfair to ignore the great story about Democratic candidate Paul Davis getting cuffed by cops after receiving a lap dance while he was at a strip club in the 1990s, when the club got searched for meth. He was single at this point, and found to be clean, but you still have to appreciate the, uhh, compromising position. It shouldn't be a big factor, but it definitely paints Davis in a different light compared to pious budget destroyer, Sam Brownback, and his campaign has made it the centerpiece of their re-election effortcs, doing whatever they can to not have to talk about Brownback's heinous recent record.

Predicted winner: Paul Davis (D), because I think moderates are going to refuse to break for Brownback. Also a Democratic Governor in Kansas isn't unheard of; Kathleen Sebelius won twice there not all that long ago.

Senate race: Ever since Chad Taylor (D) dropped out of this race, and the Kansas Supreme Court ruled that his name had to be removed from the ballot, things have looked more and more promising for a Greg Orman upset of DC-establishment hound Pat Roberts. Orman has the appeal of a political rogue who looks like Mark Ruffalo, and comes across as very sincere. He has flirted with both parties, but is more in the moderate Republican make, which benefits him as an Independent in Kansas. The interesting part of this is that he's likely to draw the moderate protest vote that is also not happy with Brownback, which won't have to worry about supporting a Senate candidate with a –D behind their name.

Wisely, the Democratic Party has stayed away from making any kind of endorsement since Taylor dropped out. At this point it would be more of a surprise if Roberts held onto the seat.

Predicted winner: Greg Orman (I)

Featured House race: Kansas at the Congressional level is the same old story. All of the seats are held by Republicans, and lacking in the drama of the statewide races, it would be very surprising to see any of them switch in 2014.

Predicted winner: Lynn Jenkins (R)

Kentucky

Governor: No race; Steve Beshear (D) is term-limited out in 2015

Senate: Mitch McConnell (R)* vs. Alison Lundergan Grimes (D)

Featured House Race: Kentucky 4 – Thomas Massie (R)* vs. Peter Newberry (D)

Analysis

"The Bluegrass State..." well, this one is impossible to bullshit around with, so here's the direct explanation: "Bluegrass is not really blue--it's green--but in the spring, bluegrass produces bluish-purple buds that when seen in large fields give a rich blue cast to the grass. Early pioneers found bluegrass growing on Kentucky's rich limestone soil, and traders began asking for the seed of the 'blue grass from Kentucky.'"

Governor: Please refer to the 2015 chapter for analysis of this race.

Senate race: Well, here we are again. Perhaps the granddaddy of this year's Senate races, Democrat and Kentucky Secretary of State Alison Grimes is trying to knock off the big kahuna, the Grand Poobah of Obstructionism, Republican Senate Minority

Leader Mitch McConnell. Despite low approval ratings, McConnell was able to hold off a Tea Party challenge from Matt Bevin in the Republican primary, and now looks strong heading into the stretch run. Grimes, while affable, has struggled to suspend the high polling numbers she earned in July and August. Democrats got an encouraging, albeit likely misleading whiff of anti-establishment Republicanism when little-known Tea Partier Dave Brat knocked off House Minority Leader Eric Cantor in a June primary. It is of course worth remembering that Cantor lost to someone even more conservative, and was widely-believed to be punished in his district for pushing immigration reform too far (to the center).

That said, Bevin was seen as the likely challenger that could have upended McConnell in a primary, and he lost to McConnell by 25%. Making it additionally hard for Grimes is that she will suffer from the same demographic issue of unionized-area Democrats vacating the state of Kentucky in recent years since the recession, which helped push Rand Paul across the finish line in 2010. Long story short, I view this race a lot like Harry Reid's in 2010. It's a romantic thought for the opposing party to knock off the big Senate gun they're so tired of putting up with, but when push comes to shove, consolidated power like that is just difficult to upend without a rock star candidate on the opposing side, (looking at you, Ashley Judd). Grimes is formidable, but barring a McConnell collapse, it's looking like his to lose.

Predicted winner: Mitch McConnell (R)

Featured House race: Thomas Massie, a career farmer and techie, was a freshman Congressman in 2012, is likely to hold onto this seat against Democratic challenger Peter Newberry. None of the other Congressional Republicans from Kentucky are seen as vulnerable this year either.

Predicted winner: Thomas Massie (R)

Louisiana

Governor: No race; Bobby Jindal (R) is term-limited out in 2015

Senate: Mary Landrieu (D)* vs. Bill Cassidy (R) vs. et al

Featured House Race: Louisiana 1 – Steve Scalise (R)* vs. Lee Dugas (D) vs. Vinny Mendoza (D) vs. Jeff Sanford (L)

Analysis

Awww, "The Pelican State" nickname was given in tribute to the official state bird, the brown pelican, which is native to Louisiana.

Governor's race: A preview of this race is included in the 2015 chapter.

Senate race: This is another huge one for Democrats, who are spending most of their time in 2014 playing defense in the Senate. It's also uniquely weird in terms of election laws; it is a blanket primary, so there are currently nine registered candidates on the ballot. If no candidate gets 50% of the vote on November 4th, there will be a runoff election held on December 6th between the top two finishers, which will likely be Landrieu and Cassidy. Republican retired Air Force Colonel Rob Maness is currently pulling around 10% of the vote away from Cassidy, who's a former physician and the Congressman for LA-6. Even with the national mood being so negative towards Obama, this would still be a big drop for Southern Democrats; Landrieu has held this seat since 1996, and has the supposed power of her influential family's last name behind her.

Predicted winner: This is just a hard call, since so much depends on how the blanket primary voting goes. The question ultimately rests in how the 3rd candidate runoff vote breaks. If the Maness vote from that goes straight to Cassidy in the general, there's no question he wins. But that campaign has to wonder why those votes are going to Maness rather than him in the first place;

Landrieu is also a moderate Democratic voter in the Senate, and has historically done well attracting independents and moderates from both sides of the aisle in general elections. A lot will happen between now and December 6th, but since I have to call it now, I think Mary Landrieu (D) hangs on, winning a big one for Democrats. I don't think Cassidy has the charisma or résumé to be a giant killer, at least not this year.

Featured House race: This will be an easy hold for Scalise (R), who just got a big promotion to House Majority Whip after Kevin McCarthy left the post to take over Eric Cantor's old job.

Don't miss: The over-affectionate Representative Vance McAllister (LA-5), the "victim" of a kiss-and-tell scandal (caught on tape!) with a married staffer earlier this year, has shrugged off Republican leadership's calls to resign, and will stand for re-election in November. Amazingly, polling looks good for him to hang around.

Maine

Governor: Paul LePage (R)* v. Mike Michaud (D) v. Eliot Cutler (I)

Senate: Susan Collins (R)* vs. Shenna Bellows (D)

Featured House race: ME-2: Emily Cain (D) vs. Bruce Poliquin (R)

Analysis

The "Pine Tree State" recognizes the white pine tree, an officially designated state symbol. Maine possesses over 17 million acres of forests!

Governor's race: Republican Paul LePage, the conservative former mayor of Waterville, won a close 2010 election, but his in-your-face conservatism hasn't done him a ton of favors with Maine voters, who tend to prefer civil discourse and moderate representation. It certainly isn't beyond Maine voters to elect an

Independent, as they sent Angus King to the Senate in 2012 following Olympia Snowe's retirement. King actually endorsed fellow Independent Eliot Cutler recently, a prominent lawyer with a history of political activism. But it looks like he'll end up with somewhere around 10-to-15% of the vote, which I think means Michaud pulls out in front. This is more likely to be a protest vote of LePage from moderate Republicans going in Cutler's direction, than disaffection directed towards Michaud, in my opinion.

Predicted winner: Mike Michaud (D)

Senate race: Susan Collins has stayed true to her moderate Republican roots, and that's made her an endangered species in an increasingly-polarized Republican Congress. But, she knows where her bread is buttered, and Maine will send her back in overwhelming fashion, possibly by a 30% margin. She deserves a lot of credit for showing that "moderate" and "bipartisanship" aren't dirty words. Shenna Bellows (D) is a good candidate in a bad race; she has done a lot of prominent work for the ACLU, and is rated as the most liberal Senate candidate this year.

Predicted winner: Susan Collins (R)

Featured House race: This is the race to fill Michaud's vacated seat. Cain, a former State Senator, has the lead in polling over former State Treasurer Bruce Poliquin, but it's still viewed as a tossup. I think this seat stays Democrat, since Michaud was popular, and the district favors it.

Predicted winner: Emily Cain (D)

Maryland

Governor: Larry Hogan (R) vs. Anthony Brown (D); Martin O'Malley (D) is term-limited out of office

Senate: No race; Barbara Mikulski (D) is up in 2016

Featured House Race: Maryland 3 – John Sarbanes (D)* vs. Charles Long (R)

Analysis

General George Washington bestowed the name "Old Line State," and thereby associated Maryland with its regular line troops, the Maryland Line, who served courageously in many Revolutionary War battles.

Governor: Martin O'Malley's Lieutenant Governor, Anthony Brown, has a big advantage in this one over Republican businessman Larry Hogan, due in part to O'Malley's popularity. Brown took some heat for the state of Maryland's Obamacare website, which had its issues, but he still has a 15 point lead in polls. Hogan gave Steny Hoyer the closest challenge of his career, but otherwise doesn't have much of a political history to sell voters on.

Predicted winner: Anthony Brown (D)

Featured House race: Sarbanes is one of the good guys...there, I said it. He even tried to introduce a campaign finance reform bill in 2012. He faces former Chemistry professor and Johns Hopkins administrator Charles Long. Sarbanes is a heavy favorite to keep this seat after three terms in Congress.

Predicted winner: John Sarbanes (D)

Massachusetts

Governor: Charlie Baker (R) vs. Martha Coakley (D); Deval Patrick (D) is term-limited out of office

Senate: Ed Markey (D)* vs. Brian Herr (R)

Featured House Race: Massachusetts 6 – Seth Moulton (D) vs. Richard Tisei (R); Incumbent John Tierney (D) loses in the primary

Analysis

Ah, good old Massachusetts. If not for the Scott Brown incident of 2010, I would say we could skip all of this, but don't look now, Martha Coakley's back and running for Governor. She won my heart in 2010 when she hilariously referred to fat Red Sock and failed video game producer Curt Schilling as "some Yankee fan," but it didn't exactly endear her to Red Sox nation, which you can safely assume is probably every male over the age of 5 in "The Bay State" (there are lots of bays). This was just one of a handful of impressive gaffes in the campaign to hold deceased liberal legend Ted Kennedy's Senate seat for Democrats; Brown ended up winning by 5%.

Governor's race: By most accounts, Coakley is running a slightly better race this time around, and has the strength of a pretty nice record as the state's Attorney General behind her. Return-candidate from 2010 Charlie Baker has to be taken seriously, even in left-friendly Massachusetts. He's closed the gap, with some unintentional assistance from Coakley, so it could really go either way. But she's the safe pick to follow in Deval Patrick's footsteps, and may get a bump from the popular Ed Markey being on the ballot too.

Predicted winner: Martha Coakley (D)

Senate race: Longtime US Rep. Ed Markey (D) won the Special Election to fill John Kerry's Senate seat in 2014. He's well-established after serving a record 36 years in the House as a respected liberal climate change and energy transition activist. He's blowing out Selectman Brian Herr and should win in November by at least 20%.

Predicted winner: Ed Markey (D)

Featured House race: MA-6 has been loaded with drama lately. Embattled nine-term US Rep. John Tierney (D) lost his primary fight with Iraq War veteran and former Marine Seth Moulton. Tierney almost lost to realtor and State Senator Richard Tisei (R) in 2012, and probably would have this year, after a long campaign of Congressional Republicans smearing Tierney as a radical leftist. It worked on some level; it weakened him to the point of losing the primary to a more moderate Moulton, who now very likely will hand Tisei another defeat. Politics can be a funny game.

Predicted winner: Seth Moulton (D)

Michigan

Governor: Rick Snyder (R)* vs. Mark Schauer (D)

Senate: Terri Lynn Land (R) vs. Gary Peters (D); Carl Levin (D) is retiring

Featured House Race: Michigan 1 – Dan Benishek (R)* vs. Jerry Cannon (D)

Analysis

"The Wolverine State" nickname came from Native Americans, who during the 1830s, compared Michigan settlers to wolverines. Some Natives, according to the story, disliked the way settlers were taking the land, because it made them think of how the voracious wolverine went after its food. Sounds about right.

Governor's race: This is a good race for a couple of reasons. Snyder is a smart politician, ex-Congressman Mark Schauer is a good challenger, and there's no lack of controversy in Snyder's record. He's best known in Democratic circles for pushing what has to be the Frank Luntz-dubbed "right-to-work" legislation, that enables public employees to be hired without joining the associated public employee union, which of course weakens unions because they lose due-payers, and the new hires receive the same salary that the union bargained for, without paying for the collective action on their behalf. It's a sly and underhanded tactic embraced by conservative Governors across the Midwest, ranging from Mitch Daniels when he was Indiana's chief executive, to Snyder, and of course Scott Walker, who threw brush on the firestorm he created by pursuing it with such zeal. That said, Snyder did it quickly, at the end of December in 2012, with Republican majorities in both statehouses, and it was much less ugly for Republicans in power than Wisconsin's protest-fest.

Ultimately, that's Snyder's greatest asset; he understands the PR game of politics well. He plays chess, while Scott Walker plays checkers. Snyder supported the declaration of bankruptcy for the city of Detroit, while refusing any federal bailout money for the city, claiming no federal money was needed for rehabilitation, which worked two-fold. Bailout money certainly wouldn't have hurt anyone in Detroit, long Michigan's most Democratic stronghold, but it sent a signal of pull yourself-up-by-your-bootstraps strength, and served an assurance that no government spending, even when it would be beneficial, made sense for a city in disarray. Love him or hate him, he's good at the game. It wouldn't be surprising at all to see "One Tough Nerd" back for another term.

Predicted winner: Rick Snyder (R)

Senate race: Peters has developed a pretty modest but consistent lead here. More mystifying is the low-profile the Land campaign has kept; there's been more commotion lately, but it's still a little strange they stayed quiet for so long. It matters that Levin is the outgoing Senator here, too; Peters is viewed as a sensible replacement for him in terms of ideology. Levin became somewhat of a Democratic institution over 6 Senate terms served, so it will certainly feel different without him representing Michigan. Land is a decent candidate as a former Michigan Secretary of State, and she may benefit from Snyder being on the ballot as well, but I think it's Peters' to lose at this point.

Predicted winner: Gary Peters (D)

Featured House race: This is a seat both parties are targeting. Benishek, a global warming-denying scientist, barely won it in 2012, but I think he'll have an easier time this year. He's facing off against legendary hardass Jerry Cannon, a retired army general, sheriff, and previous commander of detention operations at Guantanamo Bay. Talk about a law-and-order Democrat.

Predicted winner: Jerry Benishek (R), BUT THANK YOU FOR YOUR SERVICE TO OUR COUNTRY GENERAL CANNON, SIR!

Minnesota

Governor: Mark Dayton (D)* vs. Jeff Johnson (R)

Senate: Al Franken (D)* vs. Mike McFadden (R)

Featured House Race: Minnesota 8 – Rick Nolan (D)* vs. Stewart Mills (R)

Analysis

"The North Star State," or "L'Etoile du Nord" is the state motto of Minnesota; it claims to have given people a sense of direction over the course of time. It also has 12,000 lakes, but modestly claims to have only 10,000. Nice polite Midwestern folks up there, doon'tyaknowww.

Governor's race: Dayton has held in pretty well after taking the Governor's mansion for Democrats for the first time since 1986. He made a brief entrée into the sports world lately when he called on the Minnesota Vikings to deactivate star RB Adrian Peterson in light of the story that surfaced regarding Peterson's corporal punishment of one of his children. Risky, but it was the right thing to do. Johnson is a mediocre challenger, as a former state Representative, and unsuccessful candidate for Attorney General.

Dayton is likely to hold this seat unless something big happens to sink him.

Predicted winner: Mark Dayton (D)

Senate race: "I'm good enough, I'm smart enough, and doggone it, people like me!" Oh Al, it's true. Well, they liked him enough to give him a razor thin victory over incumbent Senate Norm Coleman six years ago. Political types remember how long and drawn out that legal recount battle was, as Coleman wouldn't concede for months. Franken has sort of found his voice though, as a progressive pushing campaign finance reform and other good government initiatives. He's in about the same position as Dayton; popular enough to feel secure, but nothing's for certain either.

McFadden isn't going to blow anyone out of the lake water in Minnesota, as a basic textbook conservative and head of an investment bank based in Minneapolis. Franken benefits from celebrity and name recognition, but he's also done what some wondered whether or not he was capable of, which is turn into a serious legislator with effective policymaking credentials. It's safe to say he's done that, and succeeded most Minnesotan expectations.

Predicted winner: Al Franken (D), and is it too much to ask for a Stuart Smalley appearance on the Senate floor soon?

Featured House race: This race has just been sort of strange. Nolan is a first-termer who got in with the Obama turnout of 2012, and is seen as pretty vulnerable in a barely-rated Democratic district. His opponent is long-haired faux-hippie Stewart Mills, who's choosing to talk mostly about gun rights. The hair has also gotten him some attention, to the point that he's been crowned the Brad Pitt of the Republican Party. Yes...really. His background is in small business ownership. It's anyone's seat at this point, but Mills has generated a lot more of the buzz, which I think pushes the advantage slightly over to his side.

Predicted winner: Stewart Mills (R) by a long, thin strand of fake-hippie hair

Don't miss: Crazy person and US Rep. Michele Bachmann (R) is retiring from her MN-6 seat after almost losing in 2012. She took some lumps for running a terrible Presidential campaign in 2012; with any luck, we'll get to experience it again in 2016.

Mississippi

Governor: No race; Phil Bryant (R) is eligible for re-election in 2015

Senate: Thad Cochran (R)* vs. Travis Childers (D)

Featured House Race: Mississippi 4 – Steven Palazzo (R)* vs. Matt Moore (D)

Analysis

"The Magnolia State" is a nod to the many magnolia flowers and trees found in Mississippi.

Governor's race: Please see the 2015 chapter for analysis.

Senate race: Man oh man does Thad Cochran have a story for you. He's been in this seat since 1978! I know, 36 years, pretty impressive right? Then this young gun Tea Party fella strolls up outta nowhere and says "Thad, I challenge you to a duel. You're simply too reasonable." Well this here young fella named Chris McDaniel, a state senator, beat old Thad in the Republican primary, but didn't get 50% of the vote, so there was a dag gum runoff, and wouldn't ya know it, old Thad pulled it out! But the young fella got his knickers all twisted up over it, and has charged Thad with voter fraud, for encouraging African Americans to vote in the runoff who may not have voted in the first Republican primary. Well either way, old man Thad's won that challenge, and will likely go on to handle former US Congressman and misguided Democrat Travis Childers with no problem.

Predicted winner: Thad Cochran (R)

Featured House race: My goodness, an I-talian Catholic in the Congress from the Magnolia State? It appears to be so. Palazzo won in 2010 and has been Tea Partying-it up ever since. This was actually a Democratic seat for a long time, until Gene Taylor lost it four years ago. No reason to expect any surprises here.

Predicted winner: Steven Palazzo (R)

Missouri

Governor: No race; Jay Nixon (D) is up in 2016

Senate: No race; Roy Blunt (R) is up in 2016

Featured House Race: Missouri 7 – Billy Long (R)* vs. Jim Evans (D) vs. Kevin Craig (L)

Analysis

"The Show Me State" nickname owns a somewhat unexpected etymology: it is attributed to Representative Willard Van Diver, with the intention of describing Missourians as possessing a "certain self-deprecating stubbornness," and "devotion to simple common sense." So much for the lewd assumptions the rest of us made about its origin.

Ooh boy, it was a tough summer for Governor Jay Nixon. He took a lot of heat for not acting quickly or decisively enough on what can only be called the terrible situation that unfolded in Ferguson. Whispers here and there about a Nixon run in 2016, or at least a pairing as Vice President, have taken a nosedive, at least for the time being. Nothing is impossible in Democratic politics, but those seem to have become very improbable, after he spent years grooming himself for the opportunity.

Featured House race: Auctioneer-turned-politician Billy Long is one of the good old boys you'd expect to find representin' rural Missourah. He took this seat in 2010 as a first-time candidate, and should be expected to hold onto it in a rematch from 2012 with Democratic challenger Jim Evans, who has an interesting background as a teacher and family farmer, but faces tough odds.

Predicted winner: Humdiddlyum-dooo-I-have-another-Congressional-bid-forrr-Billy Long (R)?...SOLD!

Montana

Governor: No race; Steve Bullock (D) is up in 2016

Senate: Steve Daines (R) vs. Amanda Curtis (D); John Walsh (D) is not running for re-election

Featured House Race: Montana At-Large – Ryan Zinke (R) vs. John Lewis (D)

Analysis

"The Treasure State" is a nod to the importance of mining in Montana.

Senate race: Sooo has anyone seen John Walsh's Master's thesis endnotes? Oh, the silly things that can end a career in politics. Walsh, who was hand-picked by Bullock to serve out Max Baucus's term, has been replaced by Montana State Rep. Amanda Curtis for Democrats on the ticket. Viewed as too far left for Montana, she's trailing Daines by almost 20 points in polling. Walsh was going to have a tough time with Daines, who's departing as Montana's US Congressman, but this one's all but over now. You have to wonder if former Governor Brian

Schweitzer is having second thoughts about not running for the job, even if he was too busy eyeballing a Presidential run in 2016.

Featured House race: Former State Senator Ryan Zinke (R) has a much smaller lead over Democratic aide John Lewis in this one, compared to the blowout Senate race. This is a winnable state for moderate Democrats, and Lewis is more in that mold than Curtis is. That said, Zinke will be helped by Daines' big win, adding to the argument that his old seat should stay in Republican hands.

Predicted winner: Ryan Zinke (R)

Nebraska

Governor: Pete Ricketts (R) vs. Chuck Hassebrook (D); Dave Heineman (R) is term-limited out of office

Senate: Ben Sasse (R) vs. David Domina (D); Senator Mike Johanns (R) is retiring

Featured House Race: Nebraska 2 – Lee Terry (R)* vs. Brad Ashford (D) vs. Chip Maxwell (I)

Analysis

"The Cornhusker State" is derived from the nickname for the University of Nebraska athletic teams, the "Cornhuskers," which was coined in 1900 by Charles Sherman, a sportswriter for the *Nebraska State Journal*. "Cornhuskers" replaced earlier nicknames, such as "Golden Knights," "Antelopes," and my personal favorite, "Bugeaters." The term "cornhusker" comes from the method of harvesting or "husking" corn by hand, which was common in Nebraska before the invention of husking machinery.

This looks like a clean Republican sweep; it certainly isn't the Nebraska that Bob Kerrey remembers fondly. Ricketts and Tea Party-favorite Ben Sasse are both heavy favorites. The House race is interesting because Lee Terry barely won in 2012, and has ex-State Senator Chip Maxwell running to his right. Ashford is a reasonably strong candidate for Democrats, and could sneak through if the two Republicans split the vote, but in a year like this, it's hard to see a Democrat coming out of Nebraska for the US House. The math might end up proving me wrong, but it's a long shot.

Predicted winners: Gimme a "G"! Now give me an "O"! Now let's finish it off with a "P"! What does it spell!?! G-O-P! Okay, don't count on hearing it at Nebraska football games, but at this point they might as well add it in as a cheer (Ricketts, Sasse, Terry).

Nevada

Governor: Brian Sandoval (R)* vs. Robert Goodman (D)

Senate: No race; Harry Reid (D) is up in 2016

Featured House Race: Nevada 3 – Joe Heck (R)* vs. Erin Bilbray (D)

Analysis

"The Silver State" is a brag on Nevada's large deposits of mineable silver.

Governor's race: Brian Sandoval (R) is a heavy favorite to walk in this one over former Las Vegas Economic Development Commissioner Robert Goodman. To give you an idea of how this one's shaping up, Goodman actually finished second in the Democratic primary with 25% of the vote, to "None of these candidates," which got 30%. Sandoval took over in 2010 with the Tea Party crop of Governors that have found trouble in some cases, like Rick Scott and Scott Walker, but he's won favor in Nevada by governing from the center, and being open to reasonable negotiation.

Predicted winner: Brian Sandoval (R)

Harry Reid, who survived a scare from Sharron Angle in 2010, is keeping a close eye on what's become a national spectacle in this year's Nevada Lieutenant Governor's race. This has gotten a lot of press because if the seat stays Republican, the popular Sandoval is likely to challenge Reid in 2016, and give him a pretty tough time. That race, which is an open seat because Republican Brian Krolicki is term-limited out, is Mark Hutchison (R) vs. Lucy Flores (D), with Mark Little running on the Independent ticket. I think Hutchison will benefit from the popularity of Sandoval this year, but Flores is a very able candidate, so it could really go either way.

Featured House race: Heck won a close one in 2010, and somewhat surprisingly won by 8% in 2012. This district is actually supposed to lean Democrat, but if he did that well in 2012, there's no reason to expect him to struggle this year either.

Predicted winner: Joe Heck (R)

New Hampshire

Governor: Maggie Hassan (D)* vs. Walt Havenstein (R)

Senate: Jeanne Shaheen (D)* vs. Scott Brown (R)

Featured House Race: New Hampshire 1 – Frank Guinta (R) vs. Carol Shea-Porter (D)*

Analysis

"The Granite State" came from granite being the traditional rock in New Hampshire; the state once had a large industry surrounding the quarrying of granite.

Governor's race: Hassan has a steady double-digit lead over Republican businessman Walt Havenstein. She's remained pretty popular since taking office, and shouldn't have a problem here.

Predicted winner: Maggie Hassan (D)

Senate race: Shaheen is taking on a familiar handsome face in this one; former topless model and frat boy Scott Brown has decided to roll up his carpet, throw it in the back of his pickup truck, and head for the Granite State, after losing his Massachusetts Senate seat to Elizabeth Warren in 2012. Brown has no connections to New Hampshire of real substance; he was born in Maine and spent most of the rest of his life in Massachusetts. But hey, New England is tiny right, so why not? The other big problem for Brown has been Shaheen's popularity, and what has been her competently-run campaign. I think it's hers to lose, which could still happen, but at this point it looks like a Democratic hold.

Predicted winner: Jeanne Shaheen (D)

Featured House race: Polling has swung both ways on this one; my feeling is that it's one of the seats that Democrats picked up in an Obama year, and lose in the midterms. This happened in 2010, as Guinta (who looks like a clean-shaven Artie Lange), beat Shea-Porter, who had been in the seat for two terms before then. I think Guinta repeats the feat, but there's no counting Shea-Porter out in what is a favorable ticket for Democrats statewide, with Hassan and Shaheen likely turning out a big part of the vote.

Predicted winner: Frank Guinta (R)

New Jersey

Governor: No race; Chris Christie (R) is up in 2017

Senate: Cory Booker (D)* vs. Jeff Bell (R)

Featured House Race: New Jersey 3 – Tom MacArthur (R) vs. Aimee Belgard (D)

"The Garden State," huh? Man, it really took the creative wit of Zach Braff, and charm of Natalie Portman to make Jersey look good. The official explanation of the name tells us that "distinguished citizen of Camden, Abraham Browning, stirred the pride of Jerseymen by telling them that the 'Garden State' is like a huge barrel, with both ends open, one of which is plucked by New York, and the other by Pennsylvania." Sure thing, Abe. At least "The Sopranos" took place there.

Senate race: Wait, didn't Cory Booker just win an election? He did, in October 2013, to replace longtime NJ Senator Frank Lautenberg, who passed away earlier in the year. Political nerds will remember that Governor Chris Christie also scheduled that race to be three weeks before his re-election fate was determined, a wise guy move, but hey, that's how power works right? Booker is a double-digit favorite against pouty old guy and former Reagan speechwriter Jeff Bell. He continues to be a rising Democratic star, and the Party loudmouth.

Predicted winner: THE Cory Booker (D)!!!

Featured House race: This one actually came in at a tie in a recent poll, but the suburban district makeup gives an edge to Republicans. It will come down to tactics, but I think Belgard, a lawyer, pulls off the upset over former Mayor of Randolph, Tom MacArthur, with Booker at the top of the ballot helping her out.

Predicted winner: Aimee Belgard (D)

New Mexico

Governor: Susana Martinez (R)* vs. Gary King (D)

Senate: Tom Udall (D)* vs. Allen Weh (R)

Featured House Race: New Mexico 2 – Steve Pearce (R)* vs. Roxanne Lara (D)

Analysis

The words "Land of Enchantment" adorn automobile license plates, and the phrase is used frequently in state publications to promote tourism.

Governor's race: The Land of Enchantment is seriously lacking in enchanting races this year. They're not blowouts, but I don't see any surprises jumping out either. Martinez (R) has stayed popular since she took over for Bill Richardson (D), and while she's facing a high quality candidate in state Attorney General Gary King (D), there isn't any reason to believe she should be too worried.

Predicted winner: Susana Martinez (R)

Senate race: Udall got lucky with his draw against ex-Marine and businessman Allen Weh (R), who many believe won't give him a serious race. You can imagine that his cousin Mark in Colorado is more than a little jealous about that one. Weh ran a controversial ad that involved the James Foley beheading by ISIS titled "Restore Leadership," which was criticized as coming off as both grotesque and tone deaf.

Predicted winner: Tom Udall (D)

Featured House race: Pearce won in 2010, and should be fine against former Eddy County Commissioner Roxanne Lara (D).

Predicted winner: Steve Pearce (R)

New York

Governor: Andrew Cuomo (D)* vs. Rob Astorino (R)

Senate: No race; Chuck Schumer (D) is up in 2016

Featured House Race: NY-1: Tim Bishop (D)* vs. Lee Zeldin (R)

Analysis

The name "The Empire State" is meant to recognize New York's "vast wealth and variety of resources." Geez, even the state slogan is annoyingly in your face and self-promoting. Yo come on, fuggedaboudit.

Governor's race: Incumbent and established hypocrite Andrew Cuomo (D) has found a way to turn a sure thing into a festival of misgivings for New York voters this year. After establishing a panel to investigate corruption in New York state executive offices and agencies, he decided that obviously his Governor's Office was exempt from that treatment when the panel decided it wanted to look into some of its handlings. Then when legitimately challenged in a Democratic primary, he refused to even acknowledge, much less stage a debate with his liberal opponent, Zephyr Teachout.

This is the sort of treatment one might accord to a crazy person running a write-in campaign for dog catcher, not an established, serious candidate, who happened to be a Fordham law professor. She ended up getting 35% of the primary vote. In a line that speaks for itself, Cuomo said that sometimes "debates can be a disservice to democracy." I'm not sure how refusing to debate an opponent on policy ideas enhances democracy; it seems more like standing directly in the way of it, if you ask me. But that's how it went down. His Republican challenger, radio host and Westchester County Board Executive Rob Astorino, trails Cuomo in the polls by over 20%.

Predicted winner: Andrew Cuomo (D), guardian of transparent democracy...

Featured House race: Tim Bishop (D) finds himself suddenly endangered after 12 years on the job. He won a close one in 2012, but is viewed as vulnerable against Lee Zeldin (R), a New York state senator. Zeldin is going after Bishop's support of Obamacare, but I'd be surprised to see Bishop lose this; he has a lot of campaign money on hand, and didn't have to fight the ugly primary battle that Zeldin did. And even if the district is becoming more Republican, it still leans Democrat.

Predicted winner: Tim Bishop (D)

North Carolina

Governor: No race; Pat McCrory (R) is up for re-election in 2016

Senate: Kay Hagan (D)* vs. Thom Tillis (R) vs. Sean Haugh (L)

Featured House race: North Carolina 2 – Renee Ellmers (R)* vs. Clay Aiken (D)

Analysis

Ugh, this is a long and folksy-type Southern tale, but let's try to do it justice: King Charles I of England declared the land that would be broken up into the two eventual states as "Carolina." The word Carolina originates from "Carolus", the Latin form of Charles. Because hey, why not name it after the coolest guy you know? Carolina was divided in 1710, when the southern part was called South Carolina, and the northern, older settlement, became North Carolina. Historians have stated that the principle products during the early history of North Carolina were "tar, pitch, and turpentine." After a fierce Civil War battle, General Lee heaped praise upon a regiment of North Carolina soldiers, saying "God bless the 'Tar Heel' boys," and from that, the name was born.

McCrory has in some ways been the figurehead for the Art Pope-fueled extremist Republican revolution in North Carolina over the past decade. Pope has spent millions in the state to turn it into a Koch brothers-styled playground of neo-conservatism, and is currently McCrory's Budget Director. There are signs, though, that North Carolinians are getting tired of the hijack antics.

Senate race: The first harbinger of this discontent is that Democratic incumbent Kay Hagan is about 5% ahead in polling, which a lot of people are surprised about. That number comes after a strong ad blitz was directed at Thom Tillis, the Republican Speaker of the North Carolina House. This was viewed as one of those highly vulnerable Southern seats for Democrats, after

Hagan rode in on the Obama tidal wave of 2008. She has run a strong campaign against Tillis, who is pretty easy to tie to Pope, and the Koch brother schemes of trying to dominate politics in North Carolina. (Hey guys, Will Ferrell's "The Campaign" was a comedy satire, not a serious suggestion for how to take over North Carolina and sell it to China. Stop trying to make it real). Anyway, nothing's for sure, but if Hagan keeps the same campaign tone and energy up, it looks like she'll be able to hold on in what many will consider a surprise win for Democrats.

Predicted winner: Kay Hagan (D)

Featured House race: Oh man, I really want to pick Aiken in this one. I really do. After winning the too-close-to-call Democratic primary, due to his opponent Keith Crisco crazily dying from a fatal fall while both candidates waited for the winner to be declared, Aiken has steadily hammered away at Republican incumbent Renee Ellmers. He has celebrity and a lot of campaign money going for him, but this district is just so Republican after being redistricted. I give him a lot of credit for running as an openly-gay, unapologetic liberal in what can only be considered the rural South. Ellmers looks like a lock though, a former medical assistant who won the seat in 2010, and probably holds on this year, in what will be a similar year electorally in the US House.

Predicted winner: Renee Ellmers (R)

North Dakota

Governor: No race; Jack Dalrymple (R) is up in 2016

Senate: No race; John Hoeven (R) is up in 2016

Featured House Race: North Dakota At-Large – Kevin Cramer (R)* vs. George B. Sinner (D) vs. Jack Seaman (L)

Analysis

Not exactly a haven for hippies and peaceniks, "The Peace Garden State" got its name because the International Peace Garden sits in-between the international boundary between North Dakota and Canada. Democrats scored a high-profile win in 2012, with Heidi Heitkamp taking over retiring Senator Kent Conrad's seat.

Featured House race: Cramer, a GOP activist before winning the seat in 2012, looks like an easy winner in 2014 against state senator and the bad-boy surnamed George Sinner.

Predicted winner: Kevin Cramer (R)

Ohio

Governor: John Kasich (R)* vs. Ed FitzGerald (D)

Senate: No race; Rob Portman (R) is up in 2016

Featured House Race: Ohio 6 – Bill Johnson (R)* vs. Jennifer Garrison (D)

Analysis

"The Buckeye State" received its nickname because of the many buckeye trees that once covered its hills and plains. There's a longer, folksy explanation too, but to be quite frank, ain't nobody got time for that.

Governor's race: It's really amazing that this race isn't competitive. Kasich, a former Lehman Brothers partner, (yes, the bank that started it all in 2008), attacked public employee union bargaining rights almost as soon as he got into office, in a way similar to Scott Walker. That effort was soundly rejected by an Ohio referendum vote, in one of the most historically-unionized states in America. It's also a swing state, and it should be in play, but Cuyahoga County Executive Ed FitzGerald has had problems from the start of his campaign. His most recent issue was being found alone in a car with a woman who wasn't his wife, and, somehow, without a proper driver's license. His campaign has largely committed to trying to help other state executive office candidates down-ballot, since at this point there's nothing that can be done to rectify his chances.

Predicted winner: John Kasich (R)

Featured House race: Johnson comes into this race the favorite after upsetting Charlie Wilson in 2010, and holding him off in 2012. Garrison (D) is the former Ohio House Majority Leader, and a good candidate, but the district leans Republican. The consensus also seems to be that if it didn't go Democrat in 2012, it's probably not going to switch in 2014 either.

Predicted winner: Bill Johnson (R)

Oklahoma

Governor: Mary Fallin (R)* vs. Joe Dorman (D)

Senate: Jim Inhofe (R)* vs. Matt Silverstein (D)

Senate Special: James Lankford (R) vs. Constance Johnson (D), to finish Tom Coburn's term

Featured House Race: Oklahoma 2 –Markwayne Mullin (R)* vs. Earl Everett (D) vs. Jon Douthitt (I)

Analysis

"The Sooner State" nickname has a similar origin to that of Michigan's: in 1889, the Indian Territory was opened to settlers. Thousands of people lined up on the border, and when the signal was given, they raced into the territory to claim their land. Some people went in early to claim theirs, and they became known as "Sooners"...how charming.

There won't be any shockers coming out of Oklahoma this year. It had a Democratic governor during the 2000s, but it's gone really red since. Fallin hasn't had the easiest past four years, but state Rep. Joe Dorman would need a huge break to even make this close. Fallin is bolstered by the presence of two Senate elections happening; both Inhofe and Lankford have 30% leads for the seats. Tom Coburn sort of announced his retirement out of nowhere from the US Senate, perhaps he was satisfied that he finally got the National Science Foundation to defund political science research for a year. All five of the US Congressional seats in the House are also Republican, so Mullin will not be doing too much sweating on election night either.

Predicted winners: Republicans for everyone!

Oregon

Governor: John Kitzhaber (D)* vs. Dennis Richardson (R)

Senate: Jeff Merkley (D)* vs. Monica Wehby (R)

Featured House Race: Oregon 5 – Kurt Schrader (D)* vs. Tootie Smith (R)

Analysis

"The Beaver State" nickname happened when the American Beaver was named Oregon's state animal in 1969. The beaver has been referred to as "nature's engineer," and its dam-building activities are important to natural water flow and erosion control in the state.

Governor's race: This race is supposedly getting more competitive, but I don't see it changing a whole lot before Election Day. Kitzhaber beat former NBA player and Yale grad Chris Dudley in 2010 by a point, in what was a fun race. Richardson is more of the politician type as a state rep., but the incumbent has a proven advantage in this center-left leaning state.

Predicted winner: John Kitzhaber (D)

Senate race: This had the makings of turning into a popular Republican upset pick, but M.D. Monica Wehby has struggled mightily against liberal good guy Jeff Merkley, who won in the Democratic wave of 2008. Wehby's legal issues have sort of taken front-stage, in what has turned into a tough race for her to really pick up ground in. Merkley is looking good with a double digit lead in recent polling.

Predicted winner: Jeff Merkley (D)

Featured House race: With a name like Tootie, you're probably ready for just about whatever life can throw your way. Unfortunately for her, Kurt Schrader and a Democratic district might be too much to handle.

Predicted winner: Kurt Schrader (D)

Pennsylvania

Governor: Tom Corbett (R)* vs. Tom Wolf (D)

Senate: No race; Pat Toomey (R) is up in 2016

Featured House Race: Pennsylvania 6 - Ryan Costello (R) vs. Manan Trivedi (D)

Analysis

The history behind "The Keystone State" nickname is about as self-serving as you'd probably expect. At a Jefferson Republican victory rally in October 1802, Pennsylvania was toasted as "the keystone in the federal union," and in the newspaper *Aurora* the following year the state was referred to as "the keystone in the democratic arch."

Governor's race: Ooh boy, this one was over before it started. Mister Controversial Tom Corbett has managed to dig his own grave for the most part, after delaying conviction for almost three years in the Jerry Sandusky sex abuse scandal case as Pennsylvania Attorney General, and proposing a 3% reduction in the state budget right after taking office, which oh by the way, included a 50% cut in all of the Pennsylvania state universities' operating budgets. Democratic businessman Tom Wolf will have a casual stroll to the finish line after winning a rough-and-tumble primary.

Predicted winner: Tom Wolf (D)

Featured House Race: I think this is Manan Trivedi's lucky year, after running for this seat in 2010 and 2012. It's been re-drawn to favor Republicans, but I think Corbett will be such a drag on the rest of the Republicans on the ballot this year that they end up dropping a few seats they'd hang on to in other years. PA-6 is one of those, located in suburban Philadelphia. Trivedi also boasts impressive credentials, as a medical doctor and Marine veteran. Attorney Ryan Costello has gotten Republican Party money, but Corbett is making everybody's life a little tougher this year with an -R behind their name.

Predicted winner: Manan Trivedi (D)

Rhode Island

Governor: Allan Fung (R) vs. Gina Raimondo (D); Lincoln Chafee (D) declined to run for re-election

Senate: Jack Reed (D)* vs. Mark Zaccaria (R)

Featured House Race: Rhode Island 2 – Jim Langevin (D)* vs. Rhue Reis (R)

Analysis

The "Ocean State" is a nickname used to promote tourism.

This is a Democratic stronghold, but there's definitely a race going on for Governor. Raimondo is the fiscally-conservative State Treasurer who won a tough primary, but she only leads Republican Allan Fung by a few points in recent polling. Most analysts expect her to pull away, but there's still potential for a Republican upset win here. Reed is winning his race by about 20%, and Langevin shouldn't have any issues with Reis.

Predicted winners: Raimondo, Reed, Langevin...Democrats for a change?

South Carolina

Governor: Nikki Haley (R)* vs. Vincent Sheheen (D)

Senate: Lindsey Graham (R)* vs. Brad Hutto (D)

Special Senate: Tim Scott (R)* vs. Joyce Dickerson (D), to serve the final two years of Jim DeMint's term

Featured House Race: South Carolina 2 – Joe Wilson (R)* vs. Phil Black (D) vs. Harold Geddings III (I)

Analysis

"The Palmetto State" refers to the South Carolina official state tree, the Sabal Palmetto.

Why even have general elections in South Carolina? Well, they are anyway. Haley, fancy-pants Southern gentleman Lindsey Graham, and Tim Scott all have unbeatable leads. Curiously, Jim DeMint up and left out of nowhere to take a job as the head of the Heritage Foundation a few years ago. I assume out of boredom, though he always did come off like a man who enjoyed the idea of making a name for himself in the non-profit sector. And of course, we can't forget American politics' most famous sucker for good old-fashioned decorum, Joe "YOU LIE!!!" Wilson, who will have an easy time of it returning for another fruitful term of wasting taxpayer money.

Predicted winners: Basically anyone with an –R after their name.

South Dakota

Governor: Dennis Daugaard (R)* vs. Susan Wismer (D)

Senate: Mike Rounds (R)* vs. Rick Weiland (D) vs. Larry Pressler (I)

Featured House Race: South Dakota At-Large – Kristi Noem (R)* vs. Corinna Robinson (D)

Analysis

The "Mount Rushmore State" celebrates the epic sculpture of the faces of four beloved American presidents: George Washington, Thomas Jefferson, Theodore Roosevelt, and Abraham Lincoln; they're 60-feet high and 500-feet up.

South Dakota has turned from the state that gave us George McGovern, to being in serious contention for the country's most Republican state. There hasn't been a Democratic Governor since 1974, so Daugaard, who was Mike Rounds' Lt. Governor, is likely to beat Susan Wismer by about 20%. The popular Rounds is running for the Senate seat vacated by three-term Democrat Tim Johnson; there's a strong third party presence drawing some votes off of Rounds' total in this one, but he should win. Kristi Noem (R), who drew some flak for her super cool Instagram pics with Congressman Handsome, Aaron Schock, will not have an issue with Robinson either, although it's worth mentioning that she barely won this seat in 2010.

Predicted winners: Republicans! (Daugaard, Rounds, Noem)

Note: Former US Senator Larry Pressler (I) is starting to poll very well and has Mike Rounds nervous about what looked like a walk in the park for the Senate seat. I still think it's Rounds', but there's certainly potential for that upset to happen. Pressler was a three-term US Senator before losing to Tim Johnson (D) in 1996. If he upsets Rounds, my feeling is that he'd caucus with Republicans anyway, so this isn't likely to produce a seat count change.

Tennessee

Governor: Bill Haslam (R)* vs. Charles Brown (D)

Senate: Lamar Alexander (R)* vs. Gordon Ball (D)

Featured House Race: Tennessee 4 – Scott DesJarlais (R)* vs. Lenda Sherrell (D) vs. Robert Doggart (I)

Analysis

"The Volunteer State" came from the War of 1812, when the volunteer soldiers from Tennessee, serving under General Andrew Jackson, displayed big time balls in the Battle of New Orleans.

This should all be pretty drama-free. Haslam has stayed popular and maintains a big lead over Charlie Brown. Alexander's lead is less than that, but still double digits over Ball. And winning this year's "He Got Away with It!?!" Award is TN-4 Rep. Scott DesJarlais, who has found a way to beat one of the uglier scandals in recent memory without having to resign: a physician before entering Congress, it was found in 2012 that he had extra-marital affairs with patients (probably not compliant with the Hippocratic Oath), and also demanded that his now ex-wife get abortions (though being publicly against them). He won his Republican primary by less than 100 votes, and since the district is heavily Republican, he's basically a lock to go back. Nice escape, Scotty! So much for that moral high ground, though...

Predicted winners: Republicans! (Haslam, Alexander, DesJarlais)

Texas

Governor: Greg Abbott (R) vs. Wendy Davis (D); Rick Perry (R) declined to run, and might be going to jail

Senate: John Cornyn (R)* vs. David Alameel (D)

Featured House Race: TX-23: Pete Gallego (D)* vs. Will Hurd (R)

Analysis

"The Lone Star State" name happened because a single star made an appearance on many flags for the early Republic of Texas. Some say that the star represented the wish of many Texans to achieve statehood in the United States, which sounds odd today.

Governor's race: This is a tough one; I like what the Davis candidacy has done in terms of raising women's issues, and she's a great candidate. The biggest issue for her is the fact that both wings of the Republican Party have embraced Texas Attorney General Greg Abbott. Democrats have to remember that this is still Texas...the two most recent former Governors remain George W. Bush and Rick Perry. There is that nagging desire to view Texas as turning blue by 2016, thanks to immigration trends, and I've always been kind of skeptical of it happening. The other reality here is that Davis's strong stance in support of abortion rights may be an issue for Latino voters, whom she's courting heavily, in addition to women. I think in the future it's possible for the "right kind" of Democrat to win a statewide like this in Texas, but this should be viewed as positive progress in a tough state, without a doubt.

Predicted winner: Greg Abbott (R)

Senate race: Cornyn doesn't have much of a race on his hands against businessman David Alameel (D). He should win big.

Predicted winner: John Cornyn (R)

Featured House race: This is supposedly the most competitive US House race in Texas this year. Hurd is a former CIA operative trying to knock off Gallego, who won for the first time in 2012. Gallego has a slight incumbent advantage, and there are questions regarding Hurd's fit for the district, as he's made some very conservative statements.

Predicted winner: Pete Gallego (D)

Utah

Governor: No race; Gary Herbert (R) is up in 2016

Senate: No race; Mike Lee (R) is up in 2016

Featured House Race: Utah 4 – Mia Love (R) vs. Doug Owens (D)

Analysis

"The Beehive State" has sort of an interesting story behind its nickname: "Utahans relate the beehive symbol to industry and the pioneer virtues of thrift and perseverance. The beehive was chosen as the emblem for the provisional (Mormon) State of Deseret in 1848, and was maintained on the seal of the State of Utah when it became a state in 1896."

Featured House race: Mia Love (R), former Mayor of Saratoga Springs, is an African-American Mormon and heavy favorite in this race against Doug Owens, the son of a former US Congressman. Love narrowly lost to the popular Jim Matheson (D) in 2012, but this is a hard-leaning Republican district, and with Matheson declining a 2014 run, she looks like a double-digit winner.

Predicted winner: Mia Love (R)

Vermont

Governor: Peter Shumlin (D)* vs. Scott Milne (R)

Senate: No race; Patrick Leahy (D) is up in 2016

Featured House Race: Vermont At-Large – Peter Welch (D)* vs. Mark Donka (R) vs. Cris Ericson (I) vs. Matthew Andrews (Liberty Union Party)

Analysis

"The Green Mountain State" originated from "Verd Mont," which was a name given to the Green Mountains in 1761 by the first clergyman who paid a visit to the 30,000 settlers in that country.

Predicted winners: It shouldn't surprise too many people that the state that sends Bernie Sanders to the Senate is almost without a doubt going to re-elect a Democratic Governor and Congressman. Shumlin is up by double digits over a likeable but struggling former Vermont House Representative Scott Milne. Shumlin hasn't exactly knocked the last four years out of the ballpark, either. Democratic Rep. Peter Welch should also have no problems winning back the seat he's been in since Sanders departed for the Senate in 2006.

Virginia

Governor: No race; Terry McAuliffe up in 2017

Senate: Mark Warner (D)* vs. Ed Gillespie (R)

Featured House Race: Virginia 10 - Barbara Comstock (R) vs. John Foust (D)

Analysis

"The Old Dominion State" got its name from Charles II of England, who "quartered the arms of Virginia on his shield in 1663, thus adding Virginia to his dominions of France, Ireland and Scotland"...

What? Since when do they let political consultants become Governors? Just kidding, Terry McAuliffe, more power to you I guess. Literally...

Senate race: In a matchup of boring political establishment types, incumbent Mark Warner (D) is heavily favored to win another six years. Gillespie, who worked in the Bush Jr. White House and formerly headed the RNC, has struggled to get much going against the approved-of Warner, who is a moderate Democrat viewed as a good fit for Virginia. Obviously the Bob McDonnell indictment and verdict won't be doing Republicans in Virginia many favors, but it could be worse; only Gillespie is really affected in 2014.

Predicted winner: Mark Warner (D)

Featured House race: This is one of the Arlington suburbs that's grown big over the past 30 years. The Republican advantage has slowly faded, but it's still there. Outgoing Rep. Frank Wolf retired, so the seat will be won by a newcomer, and in a more Democratic year Foust could probably pull it off. But, Comstock looks like the favorite to hold this one for the GOP.

Predicted winner: Barbara Comstock (R)

Don't miss: Former Governor Bob McDonnell is now a felon, and Eric Cantor lost his primary and now makes way more money as a lobbyist for Wall Street.

Washington

Governor: No race; Jay Inslee (D) up in 2016

Senate: No race; Patty Murray (D) up in 2016

Featured House Race: Washington 1 – Suzan DelBene (D)* vs. Pedro Celis (R)

Analysis

Happy to promote its abundant evergreen forests, and perhaps a certain recently-legalized substance as well, "The Evergreen State" is the only state named for a US President. It is also lacking in fun races in 2014, but let's take a look at our House race.

Featured House race: WA-1 features a battle between former Microsoft tech geniuses, but it's incumbent Suzan DelBene (D) who's defending the seat she won in 2012. Polls look good for her to hang on to this one, as it's a Democratic-leaning district in a reliable Left Coast state.

Predicted winner: Suzan DelBene (D)

West Virginia

Governor: No race; Earl Ray Tomblin (D) up in 2016

Senate: Shelley Moore Capito (R) vs. Natalie Tennant (D); Jay Rockefeller (D) is retiring

Featured House Race: West Virginia 3 - Nick Rahall (D)* vs. Evan Jenkins (R)

Analysis

"The Mountain State" is pretty straightforward: the Appalachian Mountains extend through the eastern portion of the state.

Senate race: Capito is the daughter of the former Governor Arch Moore of West Virginia, and has opened up a big lead over Secretary of State Natalie Tennant. This is looking like one of the lost Democratic seats, as Senator Jay Rockefeller chose to retire. Obama's unpopularity is at fever pitch in West Virginia, making life that much harder for Tennant.

Predicted winner: Shelley Moore Capito (R)

Featured House race: This one doesn't have any reason on the outside to look much different from any other House race, but it's pretty unique. Rahall, who's been in Congress for almost 40 years, is facing off against Jenkins, a former Democrat who switched parties to run against him in July. He's been trying to link Rahall to Obama and the "war on coal," while Rahall calls him a traitor and Koch brothers puppet. Jokes aside, Jenkins might be well-positioned to capture restless Democrats along with the Republican vote, creating a serious issue for Rahall.

Predicted winner: Evan Jenkins (R), but not really because he's earned it, just because it's so hard to be a Democrat in West Virginia right now.

Wisconsin

Governor: Scott Walker (R)* vs. Mary Burke (D)

Senate: No race; Ron Johnson (R) up in 2016

Featured House Race: Wisconsin 6 – Glenn Grothman (R) vs. Mark Harris (D)

Analysis

Wisconsin became "The Badger State" because the badger has been closely associated with Wisconsin since territorial days. Over the years its likeness has been incorporated in the state coat of arms, the seal, the flag, and State Capitol architecture. Wow, chill out people, it's not a penguin or some other actually cool animal.

Governor's race: Think Democrats want this one? Well, it's going to be a tough fight, for some reason. Walker has spent four years antagonizing public sector labor unions and bleeding jobs to neighboring states, but he's still hanging in there. He handed Milwaukee Mayor Tom Barrett a second head-to-head loss in the 2012 recall election, so you can't say he hasn't held his own. Mary Burke, the Democrat chosen to try to unseat King Scotty this year, has a good shot at it. A former business executive at Trek Bicycles and Madison School Board Member, Burke has impressed the powers that be into believing she's a serious contender for the job. Walker is a Koch brothers favorite though, and has openly discussed voter suppression lately, so it's hard to say where this race ends up in a lot of ways. The polling has slightly favored

Walker, but it's anyone's for the taking, and I think Democrats just plain want it more.

Predicted winner: A lot will happen before Election Day, but I think Mary Burke (D) pulls this one off. Most voters in Wisconsin aren't as conservative as Walker is, and I think his decisions and approach over the past four years have shown them that. He also simply hasn't performed that well when it comes to job growth; I don't know if being a leading national conservative voice is a big enough plus to keep a career alive in Wisconsin, like it might be in a place like Mississippi or Wyoming. Burke also provides a nice change in personality, and indicates a moderate left-center governing ideology, in what might appeal to voters as a calming departure from the right-wing adherent, Walker.

Just a side note. Wisconsin, I have always noticed from my home state of Illinois, has this apparent liberal national identity, probably because Madison is so well-publicized, and of course the Progressives that hailed from there like Robert LaFollette. But it's a state that recently has dropped Russ Feingold for Ron Johnson in the Senate, elected Scott Walker as Governor, and claims former GOP Vice Presidential candidate Paul Ryan as a Cheesehead Congressman as well. Senator Tammy Baldwin is certainly left of center, but things are much less predictably-liberal than the casual observer might think here.

Featured House race: This is an open seat that favors Republicans along Lake Michigan. State Senator Glenn Grothman shouldn't have too tough of a time with Winnebago County Executive Mark Harris (D), as the district hasn't gone for a Democrat since the 1960s. That said, Grothmann has come out with some insane statements along the campaign trail way: Andy Kroll of *Mother Jones* has documented some of these special winners, which have included badmouthing weekends, yes...weekends, like as in days off, saying sex ed could "turn kids gay," calling Planned

Parenthood racist, and claiming that "money is more important for men," in reference to the gender pay gap.

Predicted winner: Glenn Grothman (R), because this is apparently the world we live in...

Wyoming

Governor: Matt Mead (R)* vs. Pete Gosar (D)

Senate: Mike Enzi (R)* vs. Charlie Hardy (D)

Featured House Race: Wyoming At-Large – Cynthia Lummis (R)* vs. Richard Grayson (D) vs. Richard Brubaker (L)

Analysis

Known as the "Equality State" because of the rights women have traditionally enjoyed there, Wyoming women were the first in the nation to vote, serve on juries and hold public office.

Ironically, "The Equality State" is fully in the bag for Republicans, and has been for a while now. Mead, Enzi, and Lummis are all going to win handily, but it's worth mentioning that Dick Cheney's oldest spawn Liz ran a brief campaign to try to unseat the popular three-term Senator Mike Enzi in a Republican primary, and ruffled a couple of feathers in the process, between the previously-friendly families. Liz also took an unfortunate detour into criticizing her openly-gay sister Mary's marriage with her wife, which turned into a public incident on Facebook. She decided to bag the campaign in January, citing family pressures, but the nagging poll numbers that showed Enzi with a huge lead had to help that decision too. Ahhh, self-interest pursued at any price...sounds like one of the apples hasn't fallen too far from the fatherly tree.

Predicted winners: Republicans

And onto our Grand Finale...

Illinois

"The Prairie State" sets aside the third week in September each year as Illinois Prairie Week to demonstrate the value of preserving native Illinois prairies. Zzz...I'm more fond of "The Land of Lincoln" personally. He grew to national stature as a lawyer and politician my own charming Springfield, Illinois, and is buried there as well.

And for as a special treat, the Illinois song!

"Illinois" - Written by C.H. Chamberlain, Composed by Archibald Johnston

By thy rivers gently flowing, Illinois, Illinois,

O'er thy prairies verdant growing, Illinois, Illinois,

Comes an echo on the breeze.

Rustling through the leafy trees, and its mellow tones are these, Illinois, Illinois,

And its mellow tones are these, Illinois.

From a wilderness of prairies, Illinois, Illinois,

Straight thy way and never varies, Illinois, Illinois,

Till upon the inland sea,

Stands thy great commercial tree, turning all the world to thee, Illinois, Illinois,

Turning all the world to thee, Illinois.

When you heard your country calling, Illinois, Illinois,

Where the shot and shell were falling, Illinois, Illinois,

When the Southern host withdrew,

Pitting Gray against the Blue, There were none more brave than you, Illinois, Illinois,

There were none more brave than you, Illinois.

Not without thy wondrous story, Illinois, Illinois,

Can be writ the nation's glory, Illinois, Illinois,

On the record of thy years,

Abraham Lincoln's name appears, Grant and Logan, and our tears, Illinois, Illinois,

Grant and Logan, and our tears, Illinois.

Races and Analysis

People often ask me, what's the deal with Illinois? How are things so corrupt? And while I usually respond with something like, "Well what do you think they mean by Chicago-style politics?" it does seem to go deeper than just blaming the big city. Political Scientist Daniel Elazar did a study of the political cultures of the fifty US states, and it was very well-received because it all seemed so correct, and hit close to home. Illinois came in as "individualistic," which means that politicians get into politics typically to advance their careers, corruption is tolerated because politics by their nature involves dirty business, and legislating for the people often takes a back seat to amassing power, and treating government as a marketplace to get business done. It's almost like Elazar was sitting in the Illinois General Assembly gallery when he wrote this. When a certain level of corruption becomes expected, it sort of begins to exist as just another part of the system that happens. Illinois is certainly not the only place where this occurs, but it seems like it's one of the worst at hiding it, or at least recognizing it, and trying to prevent it from happening again.

Senate: Dick Durbin (D)* vs. Jim Oberweis (R)

Oh golly, this was over in March after the primary. I have to admit I've always liked Durbin: he's one of the nicer guys in big time politics, he grew up in East St. Louis, and then practiced as an attorney in Springfield, so he didn't have to go through the disgusting Chicago political machine wringer. He's a heavy favorite to win a fourth Senate term, which would make him the longest-serving US Senator in Illinois political history. He's served as Senate Majority Whip since 2007, making him the Senate's second-ranking Democrat during that time. He opposed the invasion of Iraq, and is a leader in trying to pass the DREAM Act. I'll confess that I was a summer intern for him in 2006, which is basically the equivalent of shaking a politician's hand nowadays, but either way I can't claim to be totally unbiased.

I also have a quick Durbin story; my dad and I were on a plane from Springfield to Chicago a few years ago, and Durbin was on it. The flight attendant announced they had oversold the flight and asked if anyone would volunteer to get off and take a later flight. Without hesitating, Durbin got up and exited the plane graciously, and a young boy appeared and took the seat he had vacated. So, likely the most important person on the plane, who probably needed to stay on it the most, was also the first volunteer to sacrifice his seat and his time; he really is just that kind of guy.

His opponent this year is Illinois State Senator, wealthy investor, and milk company magnate, Jim Oberweis. He's run for office six times, and after finally winning a state senate seat in 2013, he informally shed one of the better political nicknames in use today, "The Milk Dud." A recent Oberweis ad claims that Durbin "Broke Washington," which might giving the man a little too much credit. Durbin should win this by 15%, as he's stayed popular in Illinois even if Obama's approval has dwindled.

Predicted winner: Dick Durbin (D)

Governor: Pat Quinn (D)* vs. Bruce Rauner (R) vs. Chad Grimm (L)

Ugh. Where do you even start with this? Talk about having to hold your nose and pull the lever. Quinn is running for his second official term as Governor, after assuming the office when national media darling and captain of corruption Rod Blagojevich was impeached and went to jail in 2008. It is worth noting that if he wins this year, Quinn has promised to stop inflicting himself on the state of Illinois and retire in 2018, which is a charitable motion. In all actuality, Quinn hasn't been so bad. He signed same-sex marriage into law when it passed, his jobs record has been a positive, and while he initially fought the concealed carry ruling in Illinois, it took shape into a reasonably-crafted law that I think everyone is comfortable with at this point. But where success is bred in politics, one doesn't need to look too far to find mishandling as well.

Quinn is sort of a bungler when it comes to staffing issues. An early example of this came in 2010, during campaign season of course, when after giving unexplainable raises to Governor's Office staff, he blindly rationalized making up for the deficit in funds by forcing un-unionized agency managers to take furlough days, resulting in significant pay cuts to relatively innocent people (if you haven't heard, Illinois is broke and any kind of public employee raise starts a fight). This was essentially repeated in 2012, when promised retirement funds for state workers in the form of state pensions, which the Illinois General Assembly hadn't properly paid into for years, created a massive liability leading to controversial reform measures that involved revoking health care benefits and other pension guarantees. This was a middle finger to the unions from Illinois Democrats, which although probably necessary, doesn't make it any less painful for those workers who were affected. This would play into an interesting political situation in the 2014 Republican primary for Governor, but more on that later.

Quinn's real issues, the ones that are capable of sinking his re-election effort, also involve staffing problems. The Rauner campaign has hit him on dual alleged scandals, one being the misappropriation of funds from a $55 million anti-violence initiative directed at curbing crime in inner-city Chicago. The claim is that the money was used, according to the Rauner campaign, "as a slush fund," for get-out-the-vote purposes in Quinn's razor-thin 2010 gubernatorial victory over State Senator Bill Brady. The other involves patronage hiring at the Illinois Department of Transportation. That allegation stems from anti-patronage activist Michael Shakman finding alleged evidence that Quinn's chiefs of staff floated politically connected job-seekers towards IDOT, to be hired as an ostensible reward for their contributions to the Quinn effort in 2010.

To fully understand why this is a big deal, you have to remember how heavy the patronage system used to be in Illinois, thanks in large part to the Democratic machine in Chicago. This was all supposed to change in 1990, when the landmark Rutan vs. the Republican Party case, coming out of Illinois, and ruled on by the US Supreme Court, declared that no one could be removed from their state worker position (or hired to one) based on their political activity and connections. So, the charge from Shakman resulted in the firing of IDOT's director, Ann Schneider, who took the fall for everything, and it led to the removal of 58 employees hired as "staff assistants." The Quinn people skirted the issue by saying that it was up to IDOT to guarantee that no one hired violated the standards.

I was on the 2010 campaign as an intern in Springfield, and I can say that at least in my case, as an employable campaign volunteer who could have used a job afterward, no such offer was mentioned or extended to me. I cannot speak to other hires that were made, but at least in my case there was no connection presented between political activity and promise of a job. Is that fair, after volunteering your time to a cause, to find a door closed? The anti-patronage ruling says yes. But I can admit, part of this may have been my oft-conflicted relationship with then-Quinn Deputy Chief of Staff Ryan Croke.

A natural-born Party cheerleader and habitual ass-kisser, Croke took a leave that year from the Governor's Office to obnoxiously "fire the troops up" for Pat Quinn's campaign effort in September. He has been deemed too necessary to the "vital operations" of Illinois government, as Quinn's now-Chief of Staff, to engage in such petty campaigning activities this time around. Croke's ascent can be attributed to a few things: Quinn is known to prefer tall, handsome, clean-shaven white male sycophants for key "leadership" roles in his Administration, and even I can admit to being impressed with Croke's relentless desire to please his Master and Governor. But I suppose his yearly salary of $130,000 a year may be sufficient motivation as well. He somewhat humorously got promoted to his Deputy job after the woman he replaced sent a fundraising email during state work hours (between 9 am and 5 pm), and was forced to resign for engaging in politically-related activity during what is supposed to be non-partisan governing time for the good people of Illinois.

Croke then followed in equally-impressive footsteps when he took over the Chief of Staff job, after obvious sleazeball Jack Lavin departed "for an opportunity in the private sector," which of course meant turning around and lobbying the Governor's Office and General Assembly on big money issues, a practice all-too-common in politics today. The Quinn people denounced that as well of course, but it will be interesting to see where his role in the troubled anti-violence program ends up. His emails have been subpoenaed by Inspector General William Holland, who is investigating the program, and played a lead role in the eventual conviction Rod Blagojevich in his pay-to-play scheme with the

Obama Senate seat. And yet, after all of that, I'm going tell you why I'm voting for Pat Quinn in 2014.

Bruce Rauner, who is almost an actual billionaire, made basically all of his money from venture capitalism. He made a jaw-dropping $53 million last year, restructuring companies, helping them outsource work from the United States, along with finding ways to dodge taxes for himself. The University of California put out an interesting study in 2011 that supported a hypothesis that rich people, especially very wealthy people, such as Bruce, test very low on the empathy scale. That's great for self-interest, but what would it mean for the near-13 million Illinoisans who need a leader who's also capable of listening to their complaints, and understand their financial struggles?

He is a conservative, who has wavered on whether or not a federal minimum wage should even exist. He has publicly vilified unions, and big union "bosses," (since this is still the 1950s, right?) and promised to make Illinois a right-to-work state, at a time when roughly 11% of workers are unionized in the United States. With income inequality exploding so rapidly, Bruce Rauner corrected a reporter who asked him if he was "part of the 1%?" by boasting that he was "probably part of the 0.1%."

I'm sure some readers are seeing many of the same out-of-touch similarities that plagued Mitt Romney in 2012. They're there, but Romney also had one other thing going for him: real political experience. Bruce Rauner has never held elective office, and yet he thinks he'd be the perfect candidate to be governor of the state of Illinois at a time when the state's economy is in one of the most fragile, but improving recoveries, since it was admitted to the union in 1818. His go-to campaign appeal is saying he's going to "Shake up Springfield" if he wins; but everyone knows you're not supposed to shake a baby, much less the one that is the Illinois economy right now. It takes an incredible amount of arrogance to try to assert that with no experience in political leadership, or governing experience, he could just walk into the Governor's mansion, and solve all of the state's problems, based solely on the fact that he made a shitload of money in his investment banking career. Yes, in the field that not 6 years ago, brought the economies of the United States and Western Europe to their proverbial knees, by rigging the game to their benefit.

Rauner also raved about his time learning from the University of Chicago's Milton Friedman during college summers at Dartmouth, whose promotion of free-market disaster capitalism did nothing but benefit the economic elite where it was put into practice. Rauner has also bankrolled his own effort, spending $6 million of his own money to beat the qualified State Senator Kirk Dillard in the Republican primary this March. I actually voted for Dillard in that election, and would have voted for him over Quinn in the general too, because aside from being the actual best candidate for Governor, Dillard voted against the pension reform that affected so many retired state workers negatively.

He had been a federal judge, worked as popular Governor Jim Edgar's Chief of Staff, and had spent 20 years as a State Senator representing a suburban Chicago district. He's also a friendly guy, and committed "party treason" by appearing in a 2007 ad endorsing his friend and former colleague, State Senator Barack Obama, as willing to work in a bipartisan way. How dare anyone in this age of complete polarization endorse someone from the other party as being higher than a piece of shit? Well, he did it, as a favor to a friend, and it may have cost him the Governorship in 2010, when he narrowly lost the primary that year to State Senator Bill Brady. In my opinion he would have likely won that year against Quinn, because Mark Kirk, a suburban Republican similar to Dillard, beat Alexi Giannoulias for the Obama-vacated US Senate seat, who was a Chicago Democrat not a ton different from Pat Quinn. Dillard has moved on to a new job in transit authority, but he deserves a profiles in political courage award, for putting friends and workers ahead of his own career.

That said, there were things I disagreed with Dillard on too. He said, as Bruce Rauner has as well, that he opposed same-sex marriage, which became legal in Illinois in June of 2014. It just begs the question, who would a Bruce Rauner Governorship benefit, besides his own ego? Not most workers, unionized or un-unionized. Certainly not the gay community. One would hope "big business" is the answer to this question at the very least, but he hasn't even provided economic plan details that would come close to satisfying press inquiries. And certainly benefitting financially from outsourcing jobs doesn't speak well of his abilities to attract businesses or workers to Illinois. Even when you start to inspect his charitable donations, to places like his alma maters Dartmouth and Harvard, and even the University of Illinois, you get the sense that it very likely is to open future doors down the road, rather than out a giving spirit, or at the very least a tax exemption. The story about him likely clouting his daughter into the prestigious Walter Payton Prep School in Chicago makes one raise an eyebrow as to how he may use power to get what he wants, if elected Governor.

I don't mean to just beat up on Rauner. He has sort of a cool story; he's made a lot of his money on his own, even if it seems like he'd do literally anything to make it. He wears a cheap watch, seems allergic to wearing a tie, and rides a Harley. And in what I consider to be an under-covered story, he would be the first Jewish Governor elected in Illinois since Democrat Henry Horner in the 1940s. Though, I will admit that's a little suspect, since anyone who has seen that episode of Larry David's "Curb Your Enthusiasm," about Larry looking for a good divorce attorney, would know that motorcycles aren't typically popular with the Jewish community.

All that aside, I'm just not a huge fan of either of these two candidates. My time spent working on Pat Quinn's campaign in 2010 did not exactly endear me to him or the people he surrounds himself with. But Quinn makes only his Governor's salary, and has donated some of it over the years to show solidarity with people who were also struggling in a tough economy. And while he's ham-handed sometimes, I think he genuinely cares about the people of Illinois, and is concerned about the fate of the working poor and unemployed. He is a self-styled populist, who brought reforms with the Citizen's Utility Board, and in sort of a strange twist of ideology, actually brought about the shrinking of Illinois government by reducing the number of Assemblymembers, a conservative's pipe dream. He also enjoys resounding support from active duty and military veterans, who sense a genuine appreciation for their sacrifice and service, likely from his father's service in the US Navy.

Rauner's anti-union rhetoric has galvanized worker support, and delivered endorsements from the big Illinois unions, who were previously pretty upset with Illinois Democrats after pushing pension reform through. I hate using this argument, but in this case it might be true: better off with the devil you know, than the one you don't. The other factor to consider is the one involving party control: with Democrats in control of both legislature houses and the Governorship, it's been sort of a nice break from the partisan gridlock present at the federal level. Democrats will hold both houses this year, and a Governor Rauner would most likely end any kind of legislative accomplishment for at least four years. Just something to consider.

Predicted winner: I really don't know, but why should the luck of the Irish run out? It could go either way, but Pat Quinn (D) keeps getting lucky: he won by a mere 10,000 votes in the Republican wave of 2010, he held off Lisa Madigan and Bill Daley without having to go through a primary fight that would have weakened him, and cost a whole lot of money. In sort of an ironic twist of fate, he may get pushed over the finish line from the big turnout to send Senator Dick Durbin to his final term, a long-sworn rival, after Durbin dealt him a defeat in the 1996 Senate primary to fill Senator Paul Simon's seat. This isn't something that gets a lot of airtime, but people active in Illinois Democratic politics have all heard about it, and know the tension has been real over the years, even if it's faded since Quinn "got his."

Someone else to keep an eye on here is Libertarian Chad Grimm, who made it onto the ballot as a third-party candidate, which is notoriously hard to do in Illinois. Both major parties have sort of conspired to make it so, and Grimm has had to endure several legal challenges from the Rauner campaign regarding the validity of the signatures on his petition for candidacy, but he's on. Obviously a third-party presence by a Libertarian is probably going to hurt Rauner more, in the same way that a Green Party one might draw liberal votes away from Quinn. But at this point, Grimm could get a lot of protest votes from both sides. In a close race it could spell defeat for Rauner, especially vulnerable with young people who consider themselves moderate Republicans.

Lieutenant Governor: Paul Vallas (D) vs. Evelyn Sanguinetti (R)

This was a big swing-and-a-miss for the Quinn people if you ask me. After Sheila Simon announced she'd be leaving the job to pursue a different office (more on that later), the door swung wide open for Quinn to take someone from the black community in Chicago, after the 2010 decision to pass on longtime Illinois Rep. Art Turner Sr. upset more than a few. Turner was passed over in favor of Simon, who was picked to help with women and downstate Illinois (she did, at least enough to barely win). This time around, likable Illinois State Senator and Obama clone Kwame Raoul was mentioned, along with Cook County Board Executive Toni Preckwinkle. Both were passed over for Vallas, another balding, bloviating, blowhard sort in the Quinn make, a former CEO of Chicago Public Schools and self-touted educational reform genius. It was a pick that excited no one, besides maybe suburban centrists, who may have viewed Quinn as too liberal (what a great joke).

Vallas hasn't really hurt anything, but it certainly might leave some prominent black Chicago community activists scratching their heads, wondering what their big incentive to drive the black vote out for Quinn again is. Rauner has also made an effort to make some inroads with black Chicago, donating $1 million to a South Side credit union in need; some viewed it as trying to buy votes, but he delivered on needed money promised, so I'll let the reader be the judge. There has been a recent wave of black ministers endorsing Rauner for Governor over Quinn as well; it's a quiet battle, but it's the kind that can end up making a huge difference in a close election.

The Republican candidate for Lieutenant Governor, Evelyn Sanguinetti, is a suburban Councilwoman without a big history. She's attractive, but I'm not so sure she wooed voters with a sarcastic rhetorical question she asked a friend in a leaked 2013 email, which was that if she won the job, would she have to tip cows in Springfield? That's the sort of big city-slicker talking that you'd expect to hear from Chicago Democrats, not a Republican who understands the obvious importance of capturing "downstate" (what people from Chicago call the rest of Illinois that isn't Chicagoland). It's worth laughing at, but it could also be a real problem for Republicans: Rauner is from the super-wealthy suburb of Winnetka, and Sanguinetti, a fellow suburban brat, has obviously found a way to disconnect her identity from the very necessary rural and Central and Southern Illinois vote that needs to go for Republicans in order for them to win a statewide. Bill Brady ran so close in 2010 because he connected well with downstate voters; it's a demographic that might really be up in the air for Rauner, an economic royalist, and Sanguinetti, who does not sound comfortable south of I-80 whatsoever.

Predicted winner: Ever since the hilarious and stupid Scott Lee Cohen incident of 2010, (where he ran for Lieutenant Governor independent of Pat Quinn, and won, and he turned out to have some, uh, legal issues with prostitutes, and steroid rage, and his pawn business), the paired system has taken effect. So if Rauner wins, Sanguinetti does too. But since I've picked Quinn for the Governor's race, Vallas is the only option.

Attorney General: Lisa Madigan (D)* vs. Paul Schrimpf (R)

Schrimpf is this year's sacrificial goat for the Lisa Madigan shrine. She was widely viewed as a potential challenger to Quinn for the Democratic nomination for Governor, and a lot of polls showed her ahead of him. It's thought she begged off due to the conflict of interest argument gaining steam, with her as the potential Governor and her father, longtime Speaker of the Illinois House Mike Madigan, who's also the head of the state's Democratic Party, as simply too much condensed family power. Once she opted not to run, it created a logjam, as Sheila Simon was expected to run for Attorney General, but all of a sudden couldn't. Madigan's decision to stay also indirectly shook up banker and former White House Chief of Staff Bill Daley, who decided not to run against Quinn by himself. He aborted his campaign in December of 2013, with a bizarre and somewhat pathetic statement about running for office requiring more effort than he was willing to put into it. All that aside, Madigan is safe for another four years. I would watch for her to run for the Senate seat currently occupied by Mark Kirk in 2016; I thought she should have done it in 2010.

Predicted winner: Lisa Madigan (D)

Treasurer: Tom Cross (R) vs. Mike Frerichs (D)

This is very quietly an excellent race. Former Illinois House Minority Leader Tom Cross is running for the job vacated by Dan Rutherford, a Republican who gave up the seat to run for Governor. Things didn't go so great for Dan, who is facing charges for harassing an employee. I worked for a legislative session at the Illinois House and developed a lot of respect for Cross, who was a patient and dedicated leader for a minority party that pretty routinely had to accept getting stomped on. Frerichs is a really tall, sort of gawky State Senator I never grew too attached to. He went to Yale and came back to live in rural Illinois, so I guess you have to give him some credit for that. He'd be fine for the job, but then again so would Cross.

Predicted winner: I think Cross pulls this one off. Tom Cross (R)

Comptroller: Judy Baar Topinka (R)* vs. Sheila Simon (D)

This is the least competitive race on the ticket this year, for more than a few interesting reasons. Topinka is a popular moderate Republican who won the office in 2010, after losing to Blagojevich in 2006 for Governor. She also won my heart when she said that Rauner's term-limits idea was "stupid" and for the record, it's also been found to be unconstitutional. I am opposed to those simply for the reason Topinka offered: institutional knowledge and expertise cannot be developed if you kick people out of their jobs after a certain number of years. It might work at the gubernatorial level, but it's hard to see it making sense for the other executive officers, or the General Assembly. Topinka did make sort of a gaffe lately; she was caught on tape perhaps suggesting to Pat Quinn that a close relative might get a teaching job at a state university during a bill signing, which I don't know what to really say about it, but the whole thing was strange. It won't hurt her, as Simon is stuck looking like an opportunist running for a job she didn't really want in the first place, but had to settle for.

The question is begged, why would Simon drop out of the Lieutenant Governor's job anyway? Well, to make a long story short, Quinn looked like toast at the time she decided to announce she wouldn't be running with him again. Things looked pretty certain to be heading towards Lisa Madigan running and winning the Democratic primary, which would have opened the Attorney General job for Simon, a lawyer and former law professor at Southern Illinois University. It looked like the perfect fit, and I think in the future Simon would be an excellent pick for Attorney General. That is, until of course, none of it happened; Madigan stayed put as A.G., and Comptroller ended up being the only open statewide for Simon to run for. She's just as qualified as anyone to be the state's check writer, I just think beating an entrenched Topinka will be hard, and the circumstances are not right for it.

But again, the question hasn't really been answered. Why would she ditch Quinn so early into the term? Well, I can say the answer is likely twofold: the job itself is sort of nebulously defined, in that you can sort of pick and choose the policy areas you want to work in, which is nice. Aside from that, it's a little bit like Vice President, in that there isn't a whole lot to do except wait for a chance to take over for the executive, which worked out for Quinn in 2009, or use it as a launching pad to a different office. I was at the budget hearing for the executive agency offices in the General Assembly, when Simon and her Chief of Staff voiced their opinion that the office of Lieutenant Governor should be put to referendum for the voters to decide if they wanted to keep it around or not: certainly not a ringing endorsement for the importance of your job.

The other issue I was aware of, because several people I worked with on the Quinn campaign received offers to work for Simon, was that Chief of Staff DK Hirner had some, we'll call them, "creative disagreements" with how she believed the office should operate. The staff office, which is located in an entirely separate building from the Lieutenant Governor's actual office, meant that Simon was often simply not physically in the same area to oversee how business was being handled. This eventually led to a big turnover in staffing, and a lot of people left to make their own situations better. There is also an old war angle to this: Simon must be said to be firmly in Camp Durbin, as her father, former Senator Paul Simon, was Durbin's mentor, who eventually took over the vacated seat in 1996 after beating an embittered Pat Quinn in the primary. In some ways it's strange that the Quinn-Simon alliance ever happened, even as brief as it was. So, a little bit of friction likely went a long way in ending this team membership. So goes the happy family life of Illinois Democratic politics, friends.

Predicted winner: Judy Baar Topinka (R) will have no problems here, but I want to reiterate that if it ever opens up for her, I think Sheila Simon should be the next Attorney General of Illinois; she's a perfect fit for the job.

Featured House Races: It's a very poorly kept secret that the RNC is spending a lot of money in Illinois: John Boehner and Republican leadership believe they can take back a lot of the seats they won in 2010 but lost in 2012, without the Obama turnout. Let's take a look...

Illinois 8 – Tammy Duckworth (D)* vs. Larry Kaifesh (R)

Tammy Duckworth is a disabled Iraq War veteran, and the first female double amputee from the war, who currently serves in the Illinois National Guard anyway. She's also the first Asian American US Representative from Illinois. Good luck to you, Larry Kaifesh.

Predicted winner: Tammy Duckworth (D)

Illinois 10 – Brad Schneider (D)* vs. Robert Dold (R)

This is a matchup of annoying suburban types: white nerd Brad Schneider faces off against all-American jock bro and family businessman Robert Dold. He won in 2010, and Schneider beat him in 2012. My instinct is telling me it probably goes back to Republicans without the Obama bump.

Predicted winner: Robert Dold (R); how did you get my email address, Brad Schneider???

Illinois 11 – Bill Foster (D)* vs. Darlene Senger (R)

Foster is one of the few scientists who also happens to be a businessman in Congress. Senger, a former Illinois House representative, is nowhere near interesting enough of a candidate to knock him off, be it a Republican or Democratic year.

Predicted winner: Bill Foster (D)

Illinois 12 – Bill Enyart (D)* vs. Mike Bost (R)

Now things start to get tough. Enyart, a former lawyer and National Guard General, stepped in for the retiring Jerry Costello two years ago and pulled off a big win. His opponent this year is tougher though; former Illinois House Assistant Leader Mike Bost is nothing if not a character. I was present when he started screaming on the Illinois House Floor in 2012, and threw a stack of papers all over the room. The clip went viral on YouTube and got national coverage. He's a huge gun advocate and has a notorious temper, but I need to say something on his behalf.

When I was a lowly Illinois House committee clerk in 2012, he joked around with me a few times, and seemed to actually take some interest in having a conversation with me, someone who could do him absolutely no real favors. He also thanked me for the work I did in a genuine manner, something that a Representative in leadership had no reason to do unless he actually meant it. It made me feel good that no matter how small and seemingly trite the work we did was (we counted votes in committees, and routinely were treated pretty poorly), someone important took notice of the effort. Bost is a career firefighter and small businessman.

Predicted winner: This is a targeted district for both parties. It's the sort of district that needs a hawkish moderate Democrat if it's going to stay Democrat. Enyart is that, and a good politician, but Bost has an energy and charisma that I think can pull a leaning-red district to Republicans. I think it ends up close, but that Mike Bost (R) pulls it out.

Illinois 13 – Rodney Davis (R)* vs. Ann Callis (D)

Democrats have been eyeing this seat ever since longtime Rep. Tim Johnson decided to retire out of nowhere after winning his primary in 2012. Johnson, who admitted he was tired of the polarized partisanship in DC, walked away from a win, but Republicans nominated John Shimkus-staffer Rodney Davis to fill the slot, over former Miss America and Harvard Law graduate Erika Harold, who has been pretty poorly treated by the Party when it comes to challenging Davis for the seat. Davis narrowly beat physician and serial-candidate for the 13th David Gill in 2012. It's a seat that Cook Political Report says leans Democratic, but it hasn't gone that way yet. Davis' big contribution so far to Congress has been suggesting that the White House be forced to eat the same nutritionally-valued food that federal free lunch programs provide to kids who qualify for it.

[SCENE: Barack Obama "I'm sorry President Putin, Congressman Rodney Davis says we can only have this ham sandwich, juice box, and apple for lunch, not that lavish White House food anymore."

Vladimir Putin "WHAAAT! I'M HANGRY FOR REAL FOOD!" (World War 3 begins) END SCENE]

Okay, so it probably wouldn't go down like that, but come on Rod, grow up and quit with the stupid partisan games. Democrats have slated a good challenger in former Circuit Judge Ann Callis, although Davis did beat Harold in the Republican primary, so he's earned a few stripes by now. He's also had fundraisers in-district hosted by John Boehner and Paul Ryan.

Predicted winner: I think Ann Callis (D) can win this, even with the heavy Republican support for Davis. She's the right type of candidate to appeal to the University of Illinois community, too.

Illinois 17 – Cheri Bustos (D)* vs. Bobby Schilling (R)

This is another tough one. Schilling, the likable pizza businessman who pulled off a big upset of Phil Hare in 2010, is back in a rematch against former journalist Cheri Bustos, who beat him in 2012. I think this one flips like IL-10, without Obama turning out a big Democratic vote. Bustos is still at her most vulnerable after just being in Congress for one term, and she hasn't amassed a big record to stand behind.

Predicted winner: Bobby Schilling (R)

Illinois 18 – Aaron Schock (R)* vs. Darrel Miller (D)

I don't mention this race, for my home district seat, because I think it's going to be close. Schock will easily beat Miller, a farmer who switched parties to run against him. Shock is one of the Republican Party's stars, and essentially the seat is his until he doesn't want it anymore. I'm doing it for the reason everyone finds an excuse to talk about Aaron Schock.

After being outed by a gay journalist in January of 2014, he basically refused to acknowledge it, and the media agreed to not talk about it. Stephen Colbert hinted at it in his "Better Know a District" interview, and Schock played dumb until it went away, right after he took office. This is the predictable formula: it gets brought up, he refuses to answer or walks away from the interviewer, and it dies. But something happened this year, or will happen, that made things a little more complicated. A highly vulnerable Democratic Governor went up for re-election, and Schock, long viewed as the Party's best choice for that job or a Senate seat, formed an exploratory committee. Then out of nowhere, some anti-Aaron Schock ads curiously started to show up on TV. It's been speculated by journalist Rich Miller that Bruce Rauner was behind these early warning salvos, in an effort to keep Schock from entering the race. Regardless of who paid for them, it worked. Shock eased off and announced he'd be running for a fourth term in Congress, for a seat that he could never lose.

It all sounds innocent enough, and it would have been a tough primary battle. Rauner sort of came out of nowhere, and things definitely became tense between the two prominent Illinois Republicans. But Schock was probably smart to back off: fly too high, and things start to come out. Former Illinois Treasurer Dan Rutherford found this out the hard way. Rutherford, long rumored to be gay, found himself dealing with an ugly scandal involving expensive trips taken on public money with a male staffer, and then had to deal with a related-harassment allegation. That, apparently, is what happens if you try to fly too high with something to hide.

But the more curious part of this to me has been how the media handles it. If a Democrat gets wrapped up in a sex scandal, it's almost assured to hit the papers. Well...the Web, anymore, but it absolutely gets out. Schock's sexual orientation, which on one level isn't a big deal at all, does sort of become a big deal when he's forced to vote on orientation issues. He voted against amending federal hate crimes laws to include crimes where the victims were targeted on the basis of sexual orientation, gender identity, gender, and disability. He also voted against the repeal of the military's "Don't Ask, Don't Tell" policy in December of 2010.

He then voted against the use of funds for different causes if they were allocated to the defense of lawsuits related to the Defense of Marriage Act in 2012. These are, at the very least, controversial votes, and considering the unstated obvious, seem to be entirely hypocritical to his personal situation.

It just does not make sense that his sexual orientation has sort of become everyone's little secret that we all agree to keep, even when it affects public policy, because if a Democrat were to out him, it'd look like bullying and intolerance, something that wouldn't win most Democrats over. He won't speak to the media about it, and there's no sense in a Republican provoking anything out of nowhere, since he's one of the Party's stars...well, as long as he doesn't go *too* high on the elective ladder of course. I'm raising this because if Aaron Schock is gay, which I and many other people believe him to be, I think he owes it to himself to own up to who he really is. I do not do it out of malice, or a desire to see him lose his seat, or his political career. I just believe that if the Republican Party is not willing to embrace a talented politician, who embodies a lot of their core beliefs, because he is a homosexual, and he believes that he cannot own up to it for that reason, then they may not deserve his representation.

Harvey Milk, the first-elected openly gay politician and San Francisco Supervisor, once said the following:

"Every gay person must come out. As difficult as it is, you must tell your immediate family. You must tell your relatives. You must tell your friends if indeed they are your friends. You must tell the people you work with. You must tell the people in the stores you shop in. Once they realize that we indeed are their children, that we are indeed everywhere, every myth, every lie, every innuendo will be destroyed once and for all. And once you do, you will feel so much better."

Nor would Schock be the first openly-gay Republican in Congress: Steve Gunderson of Wisconsin was outed in 1994, and served until 1997. Jim Kolbe of Arizona voluntarily came out in 1996, and served until 2007. And Tammy Baldwin won a US Senate seat in 2012 as an openly-gay candidate (as a Democrat). I think the country benefits from living in a more open and understanding time now, especially in regards to sexual orientation. Even John Boehner has agreed to stand behind and fund openly-gay Republicans running for the US House this year.

And we all know you want to run for Governor or Senator soon, Aaron. No ambitious politician wins a school board position at 19, a state representative seat at the age of 23, and becomes a US Congressman at the age of 27 so they can stay in that job for the rest of their lives. So you might as well get it out of the way, and do it on your own terms right? And I'm sure you've heard Illinois passed same-sex marriage in June, in case you and a certain special somebody want to make things official.

And we all know that no straight man is capable of those eight-pack abs, great hair, and dressing as well as you do on a daily basis. So, what do you say?

—Your constituent, Anthony

Predicted winner: Aaron Schock (R)

Final 2014 Seat Total Predictions

Where does all of this leave us? Well, in the Senate, I've picked Republicans to pick up a total of 4 seats; this would put them at 49 seats. Democrats get dropped down to 48, but with 3 Independents likely caucusing with them: Angus King of Maine, Bernie Sanders of Vermont, and we will assume Greg Orman from Kansas will as well, since he is running against a Republican, this would mean that Democrats hold onto control of the Senate. But I can admit this is still very much in doubt, and it could break for

Republicans too, based on key races playing out in their favor. However, I don't see them winning the 6 to gain control; 5 is more likely, and since the count would be 50-50, Vice President Biden would be the tiebreaker to put Democrats over the top in terms of potential close votes.

The House is much more predictable, for a few reasons. Republicans already have a big majority in the House, and because of how districts are drawn, they'll likely pick up somewhere between 7-to-14 seats. The anti-Obama headwind favors them more in the House than anywhere else, so this is where gains will be made.

I think the races for Governor might surprise some people. Right now Republicans hold a big majority at 29, to 21 Democrats. But the verdicts will come in on these Tea Party Governors, and I think more unfavorably than people may suspect. I think this might look much more even after November 4th: my guess is somewhere around 25 Republicans, 24 Democrats, and 1 Independent. These executive ideologies are being put to the test this year for the first time after taking power, and I think while the US Congressional elections may be more of a referendum on Obama and the state of the country, these races for Governor will be a good measurement of the staying power of Tea Party governance. My feeling is that it has less appeal than the typical mainstream Democratic or Republican rule.

Chapter 4

2015

Gubernatorial Races:

Kentucky

Steve Beshear (D) is term-limited out of office. Democrat Jack Conway, current Attorney General of Kentucky and hyper-likable fellow St. Louis Cardinals fan, has announced his gubernatorial candidacy. Other potential Democratic candidates include banker Luther Deaton, and Daniel Mongiardo, former Lieutenant Governor.

Republican Hal Heiner, former Louisville Metro Councilman, has announced his gubernatorial candidacy. Other potential Republican candidates include Cathy Bailey, businesswoman, James Comer, Agriculture Commissioner of Kentucky, Jess Correll, banker, Ernie Fletcher, former Governor of Kentucky, and Phil Moffett, Tea Partier.

I have to admit I'm rooting for Conway in this one, who threw the ridiculous Aqua Buddha story at Rand Paul in the 2010 Senate election. I think this stays Democrat, and is his for the taking.

Louisiana

Bobby "Kenneth the Page" Jindal (R) is term-limited out of office. Republican Jay Dardenne, Lieutenant Governor of Louisiana, and David Vitter, U.S. Senator, have declared their gubernatorial candidacy. Potential Republican candidates include Russel L. Honoré, retired lieutenant general and former Commander of Joint Task Force Katrina, John Neely Kennedy, Louisiana State Treasurer, and Gerald Long, State Senator.

Democrat John Bel Edwards, Minority Leader of the Louisiana House of Representatives; Jeremy Odom, minister; and Foster

Campbell, Public Service Commissioner, have declared their gubernatorial candidacy. Potential Democratic candidates include James Bernhard, businessman; John Georges, businessman; and Mitch Landrieu, Mayor of New Orleans.

Note: Elections in Louisiana, with the exception of U.S. presidential elections, follow a variation of the open primary system called the jungle primary, as we saw in this year's Senate election. Candidates of any and all parties are listed on one ballot. Unless one candidate takes more than 50% of the vote in the first round, a run-off election is then held between the top two candidates, who may be members of the same party.

It's hard to see this going to anyone but a Republican, possibly Dardenne or annoying hooker-lover David Vitter, but Mitch Landrieu might be able to work some Louisiana Democrat magic on the race.

Mississippi

Phil Bryant (R) is eligible to run for a second term. He succeeded Republican Governor Haley Barbour in 2011 with 61% of the vote; Bryant previously served as Lieutenant Governor of Mississippi. He can claim to be the Governor when Mississippi officially entered the 21st century from the 19th, when the ratification of the 13th Amendment was finally sent in to DC by the Mississippi Secretary of State to the Federal Register, after "forgetting to send it due to a clerical error"... Bryant is currently raising money, and should be a sure thing for re-election.

State legislative elections will be held for the following in 2015: Louisiana, Mississippi, New Jersey, and Virginia.

Several cities will hold **Mayoral and municipal elections** as well. I will be focusing on Chicago and San Francisco, but other major cities having races include Dallas, TX; Denver, CO; Indianapolis, IN; Philadelphia, PA; Nashville, TN; and Columbus, OH.

Chicago, IL

"The Second City" will elect its next mayor on February 24, 2015. Incumbent Mayor Rahm "Rahmbo" Emanuel, who won the job in 2011, is eligible to run for the seat again, though he hasn't yet declared his candidacy. Currently-declared candidates include the following: Frederick Collins, Chicago police officer; Amara Enyia, urban affairs consultant; Robert Fioretti, Chicago City Alderman; William J. Kelly, political activist, columnist, and Republican candidate for Illinois Comptroller in 2010 and 2014; and Robert Shaw, former Chicago City Alderman, and former Cook County Commissioner. Fioretti is seen as the most serious challenger to Emanuel, out of that current pack. Karen Lewis, the head of the Chicago Teachers' Union, who has had several public and private battles with Emanuel over education reform, has not declared or declined to run, but is seen as a legitimate challenger to Emanuel as well.

But so far, the biggest story has not really been who's running, but who's declined to compete for the job. Popular Cook County Board President Toni Preckwinkle, effectively Chicago's second most powerful executive, announced that she would not be running in July, a surprise because she was running ahead of Emanuel in several polls at the time. Preckwinkle, a prominent leader in the African American community, was expected to challenge Emanuel, who has been criticized for his confrontational approach and New Democrat ideology, both of which have come up short, according to critics, in governing a city that has deeply-rooted racial and economic divide issues. State Senator Kwame Raoul, who was also encouraged to consider running, declined as well.

Rahm is the sort of character you couldn't invent on your own. He is a graduate of the Evanston School of Ballet; you might be able to guess where the tough guy complex came from. In high school he worked part-time at Arby's, where he severely cut his right middle finger on a meat slicer; it was later infected from swimming in Lake Michigan, and had to be partially amputated due to the severity of the infection. The irony of the most combative Democrat of our time not possessing his full right middle finger is, let's say, palpable...especially as someone who seems so reliant on it. Rahm came up through Illinois and Chicago political channels working as a staffer and fundraiser for numerous organizations.

Some of the Rahm war stories of these earlier years have passed into legend by now. I have two "favorites." Emanuel, who was working for the Democratic Congressional Campaign at the time, mailed a dead fish in a box to Democratic pollster Alan Secrest, who was late delivering polling results in 1988. And the other came on the night after the 1996 election, after a pretty successful night for Democrats and his boss. Rahm, who was angry at Democrats and Republicans who had forsaken the Clinton cause in the 1992 election, stood up at a celebratory dinner with colleagues from the campaign, and began plunging a knife into the table while he screamed off the names of said "betrayers," shouting "Dead! Dead! Dead!" after them. Y-i-k-e-s.

Mr. Intensity would go into investment banking after leaving the Clinton White House as an advisor, and quickly made millions in under three years. He worked directly with Bruce Rauner's investment firm, and saw a big payday from their work together. He would take a few other finance jobs before running for and winning Rod Blagojevich's old US Congress seat in 2002. He held that for three terms, and left to become Obama's first White House Chief of Staff in 2009. He then won election as Chicago's Mayor two years later, in 2011. The consummate political insider and establishment poster boy, Emanuel developed a big reputation in DC as a fast-talking ball buster who knew how to get his point across in a way that made you listen, or possibly cry. I don't think it's wrong to view him as the extroverted fist for

Barack Obama during that time, who has demonstrated a rather obvious distaste for the glad-handing and social trench warfare necessary for political success in DC.

So, it's interesting to see that the political celebrity surrounding Emanuel hasn't really translated into political success as an executive in the mayor's job. Rahm certainly has the pedigree and background to succeed in such a demanding job. He's a centrist Democrat with a pro-big business agenda, which fits in with the Richard Daley legacy. But Rahm hasn't commanded the same amount of respect or power that the Daleys did. Perhaps it's due to the declining influence of boss and machine politics, both locally and nationally. But I think it's a little easier than that. Being a staffer allows you to see how power operates, and observe how the game is played. But until you hold that real executive job, I think there has to be an obvious learning curve period.

Both Daleys were certainly no strangers to controversy. But you must grant them this; both of them were intimately involved with Chicago politics and municipal administration for most of their careers. Rahm effectively grew up in the suburbs, and when it became career time, spent a whole lot of time in DC; he was initially ruled ineligible to run for Mayor because he hadn't lived in the city for more than a year, a decision that had to be overturned by the Illinois Supreme Court. No one is accusing him of not being "Chicago enough," but there are certainly differences between his background, and those who grew up in the city itself, and know a much different world inside those city borders than he does.

You have to wonder what kept Preckwinkle out of this race, and hope that it wasn't some sort of heavy-handed threat. Fioretti is mounting an aggressive effort, and judging by the past Emanuel-CPS showdowns, a Karen Lewis run would be entertaining, and I think hers is an important voice that needs to be heard, on the behalf of working people and educators. With Preckwinkle out,

Rahm is probably the favorite to win re-election, but he's had to face a steep learning curve on the job over the past few years. I think he's a better candidate and mayor for it, but sometimes it's nice to see those DC big shots struggle when they come home, every once in a while.

San Francisco, CA

Ed Lee took over as Mayor of San Francisco in 2011 for the departing Gavin Newsom, who left to serve as Lieutenant Governor in Jerry Brown's Administration. Lee was selected 10-1 by the San Francisco Board of Supervisors to finish out the remaining ten months of Newsom's term, due in part to his promise not to seek election in November. He was City Administrator prior to being appointed mayor, and serves as the first Chinese and Asian American mayor in the city's history. Following a "Run Ed Run" campaign by local political heavy-hitters, he decided to enter the mayor's race in 2011, and became the hands-down favorite for re-election.

I did some precinct walking for San Francisco Supervisor Board President David Chiu in that election, who ended up finishing fourth overall. Chiu is considered a sure thing to replace termed-out Assemblyman Tom Ammiano, in this year's election for the California statehouse. Interestingly, Ammiano has drawn some high marks in a recent poll for San Francisco Mayor against Ed Lee, as liberals and progressives are feeling around for potential candidates to run against Lee in 2015. City Attorney Dennis Herrera, Supervisor John Avalos, and former Mayor Art Agnos are all seen as potential challengers to Lee, who still enjoys a reasonably high popularity rating.

But that's not to say Ed Lee, and San Francisco, don't have some issues to resolve. Lee was implicated lately in the bizarre State Senator Leland Yee gun-running scandal in a lawsuit filed on behalf of Raymond "Shrimp Boy" (great nickname) Chow. Lee is most likely clean, according to reports, but either way it's the sort of thing he probably would prefer not be associated with his good name. Yee is likely to get most of the blame, at least politically. The other obvious issue for Lee is the affordability crisis in San Francisco, brought on by the boom in high-paying finance, business consulting, and tech jobs, resulting in wealthy yuppies competing against each other for limited living arrangements. This crunch, while great for Bay Area landlords and realtors, has raised questions about where San Francisco is heading, in a city-wide identity crisis that looks more like "Manhattanization" than anything else at this point.

The wariness of the drive towards construction of luxury housing and favoring downtown corporate interests was a common theme in Harvey Milk's campaigns, long the loudest advocate of keeping San Francisco's neighborhoods the affordable center of culture, and the lifeblood of the City by the Bay. Milk saw downtown business interests taking over even in the late 1970s, and would likely be shocked by the current housing crisis that's hit the whole Bay Area, not just San Francisco. Here he is, in vintage form, on the topic:

"Let's make no mistake about this: The American Dream starts with the neighborhoods. If we wish to rebuild our cities, we must first rebuild our neighborhoods. And to do that, we must understand that the quality of life is more important than the standard of living. To sit on the front steps--whether it's a veranda in a small town or a concrete stoop in a big city--and to talk to our neighbors, is infinitely more important than to huddle on the living-room lounger and watch a make-believe world in not-quite living color."

It's becoming cliché already, but I know I'm not the only person dismayed to hear about a $100,000 annual income requirement to rent an apartment, or the deplorable installation of big brass spikes outside of expensive apartment buildings designed to prevent the less fortunate from sleeping there overnight, who might force the new San Francisco wealthy to deal with the uncomfortable reality of being the beneficiaries of exploding income inequality growth.

A city that used to be the haven for those wishing to break new ground, and establish hope for a new life, is becoming increasingly out of reach for more and more Americans who might want to try their luck, roll the dice, and take that path. And I think Harvey Milk, who followed just that route to San Francisco, in an effort to gain freedom from gay persecution and start a new life, would be disappointed to hear it's developed this way. Ed Lee isn't really to blame for things becoming so expensive; but it certainly makes him vulnerable to a progressive like Tom Ammiano, who sees and understands what's been happening to the neighborhoods of San Francisco. The next election for the San Francisco Mayoralty will be held on November 3, 2015.

Sorting Out the Obama Legacy

We are starting to enter into the time for Barack Obama when you have a reasonably large sample size of what he's accomplished, what he hasn't, and where his place in history might be settling. His critics are many, and detractors have a long list of issues that can rightly be picked. But I think to really assess where he is, you have to start at the beginning of his effort for the office. This was the campaign that changed campaigning forever; it raised a record amount of money through small donations, it got people energized and believing in politics again, and it offered hope for the future of the country, something that was in short supply after eight years of a Bush agenda that seemed completely uninterested in listening to Americans on policy matters.

I realize people are tired of the blame throwing, but history does not unravel in a vacuum either. George W. Bush assumed the office in 2001 with a budget surplus, a relatively peaceful world, and a stable economy. Can you really say the same table was set for Barack Obama? Hardly. He assumed control of the reins at a time when the world economy was in free fall, due in large part to the deregulation agenda of Alan Greenspan and other neoconservatives, who believed unfailingly in the corrective invisible hand to regulate markets, despite the numerous bubbles that had popped before the big one exploded. He was mired in a massive budget hole from the start, thanks to irresponsible Bush-era tax cuts, massive spending on the War in Iraq, and the related contractors who gouged the taxpayer with no-bid contracts. So yes, perhaps Americans needed to hear a positive, hopeful message after 8 years of Bush hand-tying. The other aspect to the set-the-sights-high campaign of 2008 was the trainwreck of John Kerry's campaign four years prior; you can understand Democrats wanting to sell high rather than blowing another one. And it was still a clean campaign, something you cannot say about how the Bush people ran theirs (ask John McCain about those ethics).

So, okay. Obama gets in, thanks to being a great speaker and better campaigner: easily on the level of a John Kennedy, a Ronald Reagan, or a Bill Clinton, if not the best of those four in the television era. But here is where the real problem begins: after winning a landslide and both Congressional chambers on a liberal, change agenda, Democrats looked backwards. They looked in the rear-view mirror, nervous about having power again, and decided to reach back to the Clinton Presidency. And then they said, "Can we screw this up in the same way we did then?" Instead of following through on progressive ideas, like closing Guantanamo Bay, reining in the surveillance state, and pushing a big public works jobs and infrastructure program, with all of the power amassed on their side, Democrats chose to "fix" healthcare.

Attribute it to Rahm being pissed off that the Clinton people were disorganized and dropped that specific ball in 1993, or whatever you like, but while it was a worthwhile fight to immediately pick, it was also probably the most divisive policy fight to start out with. Rather than focus on tangible, quick results, like a big jobs program, that would have addressed public desperation with the taking economy, the decision was made to take on one of the most entrenched and powerful industries in DC, and to fight the kind of battle that only ensured a total and immediate drain of the Administration's political capital, and a flurry of public confusion about the final program, that landed somewhere in the hazy middle of reform and regression. The muddled details made both sides feel like they were getting the short end of the deal, no one from the Administration wanted to step up and explain it to the public, and it wasn't going to take place for four years.

This struggle is eerily similar to the Clinton mishandling of it, without even passing anything, that led to the Republican Revolution in 1994 based on the Contract with America. You can easily see the parallel between that election, which netted Republicans a 54-seat gain, and the energy behind Tea Party Republicans that took over an astounding 63 House seats in the 2010 election. Clinton was forced to triangulate his way back to mainstream popularity, and abandon his liberal goals, in much the same way Obama has. Both gave in to deficit hawks complaining about big government spending, after both had Republican predecessors who exploded the deficit with almost pornographic levels of military spending.

It also must be said that the lack of Republican creativity in opposition of both Presidents has been staggering. Both Houses embarked on government shutdowns in 1995 and 2013; both brought lawsuits against sitting Presidents, Clinton for the Lewinksy scandal, and Obama for the absolutely ridiculous reason of "not enforcing the law" by delaying the healthcare coverage mandate for employers in Obamacare, after House Republicans voted to repeal the law 50 times. All of the aforementioned stunts mostly backfired on Republicans, as the public sided with the President in each matter (the Boehner lawsuit is still up in the air, but it's not looking great so far). However, there is one key difference between the Clinton and Obama Presidencies, and it's the level of polarization Obama must face that Clinton simply didn't have to deal with.

It is foolish, and perhaps even a disservice to responsible analysis, to ignore the fact that Clinton, as a white male from Arkansas, with a Southern accent, faced a more restrained, and less take-no-prisoners approach, than Barack Obama has, as an African American man from really everywhere, but most recently before he became President, Chicago, Illinois. Things like refusing to raise the debt-ceiling at any cost were not tactics that Clinton, for the most part, had to put up with. There was a level of civility in discourse between parties that evaporated. You have Joe Wilson and Samuel Alito yelling at the President during State of the Union speeches; when did this happen to Bill Clinton or either Bush?

Yes, Obama has disappointed liberals who dreamt of more. But it isn't fair to blame him entirely for the struggling. There have been wins: Osama bin-Laden was ascertained and killed for his role in the 9/11 attacks. The level of uninsured Americans has dropped by about 7-10%; even if the program isn't perfect, it's a step in the right direction for a more fair and patient-friendly healthcare system. Unemployment is down 4% since reaching its peak in 2009. Sure, there have been missteps. The alarming level to which Americans and our allies were and are being wirelessly observed by the NSA, the use of drones in warfare, the ongoing conflicts in the Middle East, the lack of action on immigration, are all very important problems that need to be acted on.

But there is a big difference between being a failure as a President, and serving as a responsible stabilizer, who made the best of a situation that became awfully difficult because of a few early missteps. I remember the hopeless, lost feeling of the Bush years; the knowledge that nothing you believed or cared about would be even close to addressed. This is the essence of the misunderstanding of George W. Bush as a responsible leader; it is easy to look confident, and like you're leading people, when your agenda is not up for debate at all, whatsoever. When the inconvenience of facts or reality get in the way, and you ignore them because it weakens your views, it is not leadership. It's stubbornness, and an active refusal to include voters in your policymaking process. I don't think you can accuse Barack Obama of this; he may not be the strong, forceful leader that a Teddy Roosevelt was, but he is open to working hard, representing the country with sincere dignity, and he listens to both sides of an argument before making a decision. He hasn't had a morality shortfall or scandal like the one Bill Clinton put the country through. He has, by several measures, been more fiscally restrained than Ronald Reagan was. Don't get me wrong, he hasn't been perfect. But I think history will be more kind to the Obama legacy than we are apt to believe right now. And with all the problems America and the world are facing right now, it's certainly too early to give up on him now.

Potential Presidential Primary Candidates

The other part of 2015 is, of course, much more geared towards 2016. Then-candidate Obama declared his intention to run for President in February (!) of 2007. Yes, a 21 month-long campaign. His 2012 opponent, Mitt Romney, declared his eligibility in June of 2011. Not as early, but still 17 months. So while yes it's still early, we probably need to accept the inevitability of this happening soon, and start to review some potential Presidents. All complaining aside, I think this will be an exciting and surprising process, with both parties seeking to reinvent themselves in some big ways.

It's no secret that campaigns have getting longer, partially because the primaries have overtaken the typical convention nominating process. For comparison, JFK declared his candidacy in January of 1960. Reagan kicked his effort off for 1980 in November of 1979. If the political class wants Americans to hate politics less, setting a maximum campaign length might be something to consider.

2016's Possible Contenders

The fatigue factor is an interesting element in who becomes the next President throughout recent electoral history: Americans,

117

tired of Jimmy Carter, an earnest and folksy Southern Governor, turned to a Hollywood star in Ronald Reagan in 1980; unsatisfied with George H.W. Bush, a mild-mannered Northeasterner, they broke for the Southern charm, youth, and law-and-order appeal of Bill Clinton in 1992; fed up with George W. Bush's Southern cowboy bluster, voters flocked to elect a smart and charismatic African American from all over the world in 2008. If Obama fatigue lingers, it may be ripe time to elect the first female President, or head back towards Obama's stated ideological opposite; a white, conservative male. Besides, in a time when TV and the internet media puts the President in your face constantly, you have to choose wisely; we probably have to put up with this new one for eight years again, if the recent past is any indication.

Democrats

Bernie Sanders – Bernie sounds like he may be the most poised to run out of anyone, thereby the first spot goes to him. An Independent Senator (well, really a Democratic Socialist) from Vermont, he looks ready to take over the eccentric, idealistic, lovable spot vacated by Rep. Dennis Kucinich. But make no mistake about it: Bernie says what he means, and means what he says. This unusual level of honesty and concern for the country will probably come off as strange, and in the past would have likely rendered him unelectable, as is prone to happen with people like him (see Ralph Nader). But I'm getting the impression from recent reports that talk of a candidacy by Sanders is putting establishment types like Hillary Clinton on edge. People are fed up, and might be more willing to listen to the old guy with the goofy hair saying progressive things, passionately. Even if not, I guess on the plus side, if any Tea Party member wants to scream "Socialist!" at him, they'd sort of be right about it for once, after years of yelling it at centrist capitalist-elitist Barack Obama. Sanders is expected to run as a Democrat if he does, since certain obvious advantages are accorded to members of the two main parties (like being allowed to participate in primary debates).

Hillary Clinton – Who? Jesus, kidding, relax. Long-viewed as the heiress to the throne after narrowly losing the 2008 primary battle to Barack Obama, Mrs. Clinton starts as the establishment's candidate-to-beat. You certainly can't second guess her pedigree: First Lady for eight years, a US Senator from New York, and most-recently, Secretary of State. But even the most rabid Clinton fan has to admit there's some baggage with this candidacy: between all of the old Clinton stories, and a not uncontroversial term as the United States' head diplomat, there will be concerns to address in this candidacy. Not to mention the fact that her avowed New Democrat, hawkish, Wall Street-friendly ideology puts her right in the political Center after 8 years of disappointing Obama centrism; it's not hard to imagine someone, almost anyone else listed, being able to drive a truck through the Left side of her positions, and beating her to the finish line again. She still starts as the favorite, but I believe it's much less locked up than most Hillary fans want to believe.

Elizabeth Warren – As the spokeswoman for resurgent Progressivism, Elizabeth Warren has, fairly or unfairly, been viewed as the main liberal competitor for Hillary Clinton. Her building of the Consumer Financial Protection Bureau, from the ground up, grew her name recognition in DC. That reputation spread nationally after defeating the professionally-handsome Scott Brown for his Massachusetts US Senate seat in 2012. Detractors will point to her lack of time on the establishment scene in as a possible negative, but no one can deny she has an argumentative force and charisma that makes people take notice of her leadership ability. She has denied any interest in running, but things can turn around quickly if the circumstances are right.

Jerry Brown – Brown is an interesting case right now, because he's presided over California's recent financial comeback; the Jerry Brown Turn-Around, if you will. He's going to win a landmark fourth term as California Governor by a wide margin, and is one of the few politicians in America who can take credit for actually doing something well recently. He's not a young man anymore at

76, but as someone who historically loves to run for President, (he ran in '76, '80, and '92), it's hard to see him taking a pass on what will likely be his final opportunity; and especially since he's earned the right to do so, after building up an impressive record lately.

Joe Biden – I have to admit I've always had a soft spot for Biden. He may be gaffe prone, but hey, who could be more gaffe prone than George W. Bush, and he won right? Well, sort of. Anyway, Biden is actually Vice President right now, and I think deserves some serious attention for the job, since obviously Barack Obama picked him to be next-in-line. In all seriousness, he has some excellent credentials as a 36-year Senator from Delaware and previous Chairman of the Senate Committee on Foreign Relations. And, after Barack Obama basically fainted in that first 2012 debate in Denver against Mitt Romney, who showed up to deliver the straight talk and take the momentum back for Democrats? You got it, Uncle Joey. He'll definitely run, there's no doubt about that.

Al Gore – Talk about being owed something. I've heard whispers that Gore has been thinking about 2016, but no concrete evidence of it. The former Vice President, Nobel Prize winner, and global warming activist still has a top-tier mind for policy, but it's unclear if he's interested in getting back into the game again. I think there'd be a lot of people rooting for him if he decided to.

Dick Durbin – I'm throwing Durbin in here perhaps as a pipedream of mine; he's never mentioned running, though he was rumored to be on Al Gore's short list for Vice President in 2000. I think he'd be a competitive candidate for a few reasons: he's pretty well-liked, has been the #2 Democrat in the Senate for 7 years now, and is an intelligent and skilled debater, certainly a plus in the primary wringer. And his Senate seat will be safe after what projects to be a reasonably big win for his fourth term. Not a bad way to top off a long career in politics, perhaps?

Brian Schweitzer – Schweitzer, a former Governor of conventionally-red state Montana, has sort of groomed himself for

2016. But he may have made a big mistake by not pursuing the open Senate seat vacated by Max Baucus and then John Walsh. His low name recognition nationally is not going to do him any favors, and in a year the Democrats really needed a strong candidate to possibly keep the Walsh seat and hold the Senate majority, he didn't step up for it. He's had some other issues of late that may just make a 2016 run not feasible.

Martin O'Malley – This guy is a very intriguing dark horse, and no I'm not referencing the tan. O'Malley quietly was a very popular Governor of Maryland until his term-limit came up this year. He gave a good speech at the 2012 Democratic Convention, and is doing some yeoman work in Iowa already. Don't be surprised if he comes out of nowhere to be competitive in the early primaries, and possibly beyond.

Andrew Cuomo – New York's Governor pretty obviously has the ambition to run for President. Unfortunately, he doesn't have the likability factor going for him in the way his father Mario did. He's also raised some eyebrows with how he's handled ethics inquiries, and his dismissal of a valid primary opponent this year without agreeing to a debate. He'll win big in November, but it's hard to say how Cuomo would be received on the national stage.

Michael Bloomberg – The former Mayor of New York City is sort of difficult to assign a party to. He was, as most are, an Independent while he served as mayor, and is a very wealthy man who used to be a Republican. But his recent stands against gun violence, and consumer protection efforts (read: the sodas are too big and sugary), put him sort of in Democrat territory now. He'd be an interesting candidate and a moderate voice, if he chose to run.

Republicans

Chris Christie – Well, the big guy got some good news lately. He was found to not be directly involved in Bridgegate – which is still just such a Jersey thing to even have happened. He's been on a rollercoaster ride the past few years: his approval rating soared with handling Superstorm Sandy well, and he looked Presidential in shots with Obama, when he delivered relief supplies at ground-zero. He then made the Republican establishment upset when he didn't really get behind then-candidate Mitt Romney, which won him even more middle ground, and then the wise guy bridge scandal news broke and knocked him back down, where for ten months he's been trying to prove he's not a vindictive bully. But, he seems to be on the rebound, as long as nothing else too ugly comes out for a while.

He has sort of a likable and straight-talk persona that you can see would appeal to blue state voters, which is how someone as conservative as he is has won in New Jersey twice. And even I'll go to bat for him: give the guy a break on the weight thing, it's not like he's running for marathoner-in-chief, right? That's why politics is great: it's like baseball, you can be fat and still be a success. Though, if he did end up winning, think of the reality TV show possibilities: *West Wing* meets *Biggest Loser*? Talk about a sure-fire hit, NBC! Anyway, I'm certainly not anointing him, but he's probably back at the top of the Republican dogpile for 2016...to the chagrin of everyone trapped beneath him.

Rand Paul – Paul is the most intriguing member of the Republican Party for several reasons right now. He's standoffish, unpredictable, a Libertarian, and the inheritor of his father's highly-energized following. Ron Paul was a maverick in the Republican Party, and the establishment and media treated him that way. But you have to give the old guy credit, he stuck to his guns and delivered his message, which conflicted with mainstream Republicanism about half the time. It will be interesting to see if that sort of blackballing happens to Rand as well. He has the youth and charisma his father lacked, when Ron became really popular. But how will the Libertarian message play to primary voters? It's never resonated loudly enough to become a serious player in elections in the past. Can Paul change that? It should be interesting to watch unfold.

Scott Walker – Ohhh, Scotty. You can't get much more polarizing than this guy, which of course might actually be an asset in the Republican primaries anymore. Walker has one big problem though; he never completed his bachelor's degree at Marquette. The silver lining of possibly losing his race for Governor of Wisconsin in 2014 is that, if it happened, he could go back to college, rush a frat, likely win the house's president job, get even more executive experience that way, finish his degree, and come out of it ready to win those 2016 primaries! It sounds like he's running for President, win or lose in 2014. He's a Koch brothers favorite, so you can't count him out of it, at least financially.

John Kasich – A conservative governor from the swing state of Ohio, Kasich is looking good in his re-election bid against walking ball of political flames Ed FitzGerald. The margin of victory in that race could be key for Kasich; in what should have been a tough race, if he wins by more than 15%, it looks like a mandate after his controversial first term, and he immediately becomes a serious contender for 2016.

Ted Cruz – Ugh, just next. Next!

Marco Rubio – A Tea Party darling in 2010, Rubio has sort of seen his status trickle down slowly. He hasn't taken a lead in immigration reform, and the latest image most Americans have of him in their heads is that bizarre grasp for a drink of water during his State of the Union rebuttal in 2013. But, he's still handsome and Latino, so there's a good chance he'll run anyway.

Jeb Bush – Oh God, another Bush. Though I will admit, Jeb comes off a lot more capable and earnest than W. ever did. The former Governor of Florida can never be counted out, thanks to his family's history and connections, but it would be surprising to see him really take off after how his brother's Presidency ended. Something about a father and two sons being President from the same family seems awfully...undemocratic.

Bobby Jindal – I have to confess, I actually forgot about this guy when making this list the first time. He served his full two terms as Governor of Louisiana, and will likely run in 2016, but he just sort of lacks the "wow" factor that gets anyone too excited. He came across as too Kenneth the Page, the over-polite Southern staff toady from the sitcom "30 Rock" in his rebuttal to an Obama State of the Union speech in 2009, and recently looked like sort of a doofus trying to fight with Stephen Colbert on Twitter. He might be able to answer the call for Republicans later on, but not running for President in 2012 limits him in 2016, in my opinion.

Tim Pawlenty – The former white bread Governor of Minnesota may have left the dance a little too early in 2012. A likable Midwestern fella, Pawlenty dropped out early after lackluster polling, but may have had a shot at pulling off the everyman card against Mitt Romney, and potentially Barack Obama in the general. His moment may have passed.

Jon Hunstman – 2016 was in a lot of ways supposed to be Hunstman's year. After a slipshod campaign effort and late entrance into the 2012 primaries, the former Utah Governor didn't curry a lot of favor with Republican primary voters. He served as Barack Obama's Ambassador to China, and as a moderate Republican, didn't connect with Republican primary voters. It'd be a surprise to see him run again, but I guess you never know.

Michele Bachmann – After what can only be called a disastrous effort for President in 2012, Bachmann almost lost her House seat afterward too. She's retiring from the House this year, likely to avoid a potential loss. She can't be considered a serious candidate for 2016, but that hasn't stopped her from running in the past.

Ben Carson – This whole rise to fame has been sort of strange and out of left-field for African American high-profile physician Ben Carson. He delivered a rousing speech at a conservative prayer breakfast and it led to him becoming sort of a Tea Party hero.

Despite not having any elective experience, he may end up in the fray anyway. Fox News' Chris Wallace recently asked him why he thinks he'd be any better at the job than Barack Obama, saying he doesn't even have any elective experience to suggest he could handle being President: you have to give it to Fox, when they aren't on your side, even as a Republican, they let you know it.

Rick Perry – Everything was looking good for another Rick Perry Makes Love to America Tour in 2016; he decided to retire as Governor of Texas in 2014, which would have freed him up to do some early work in Iowa. He had campaigned in blue states to try to steal companies away, dangling a low corporate tax rate and that hot, muggy Texas weather. And he had even debuted his new smart guy glasses. Until...it didn't look so good anymore. He was indicted for threatening to veto funds to a specific Texas state agency if a Perry-antagonist and head of that agency wasn't fired, and this ended up being a pretty serious abuse of power issue. He may be facing a trial, and 2016 looks done-for.

Mike Huckabee – Huck went from being a feel-good candidate in 2008, to just another run-of-the-mill hack with a Fox News show afterward. Not sure if he's serious about 2016, but he does fill a constituency voice for the Party's Southern Christians.

Rick Santorum – Well "The Rooster" will probably be back after a "meh" but not so bad showing in the 2012 primaries. The highlight of those was obviously Newt Gingrich announcing his plan to launch a moon colony for wealthy people (one can only hope he'd be an early resident), but Santorum filled up the void left in the Christian Right coalition that Huckabee left by not running. Thanks to Dan Savage for finally defining for us what "Santorum" really means.

Mitt Romney – Mitt has indicated having no interest in running in 2016, and it's not likely he'd be a popular pick to win again, but he was the guy in 2012, and that means something. He didn't run a terrible race, or get blown out, but he did show Republicans where they're vulnerable. Selecting someone a little "closer to the ground" should be tops on Republicans' list in 2016; the really rich guy candidacy is a hard sell right now, especially with the Wall Street ties he had.

Condoleezza Rice – I'm including Rice because I've always kind of wondered why she doesn't get more attention for President from Republicans. Well, I mean, there are some possible, shall we say, "demographic hang-ups," that could work against her in the Republican primary. And her career work in academia has become all but anathema when it comes to "electing leadership" nowadays, for whatever reason. She served as the first female Republican Secretary of State, and while she might conjure traumatic flashbacks to images of Bush foreign policy, she's incredibly smart, well-versed in international relations, and seems like she'd be a formidable candidate. Just my impression.

Paul Ryan – Ryan got some exposure in 2012 that doesn't really hurt him if he's considering a 2016 run. He has strong views on a lot of social issues that could be a problem for him in the general election, but he's younger than most big name Republicans, and has that sort of "aw, shucks" Midwestern politeness that plays well nationally. His budget-writing duties have led him to be labeled the intellectual force behind the modern Republican Party. He'd be one to watch if he decides to run in 2016.

Chapter 5

Current Issues...Oh, we got some current issues, all right.

Same-Sex Marriage

I think when discussing why gay marriage has become such a no-brainer issue lately, there are a few big reasons. First of all, religious opposition, while present, has diminished greatly from the forefront of the argument. Rumors of a 50% heterosexual divorce rate have to have helped out too; it's doubtful that same-sex couples could be much worse at staying married than straight couples. But there are deeper reasons here, too. There's no doubt that more same-sex couples would help the adoption system find a match for more children who need a good home. And scientific studies are coming in saying that children who are raised by same-sex couples are more likely to be more open-minded and understanding of diversity in general, which is an obvious positive.

Millennials are especially supportive because I think we view this issue as the children of the divorce generation, in some respects. There is also a strange sort of Jim Crow type of discrimination in terms of preventing grown, adult citizens of the United States from marrying the person that they naturally love. The tortured myths that have been adopted and discarded about the gay community over the past fifty years: ranging from that they were all pedophiles, to the absurd notion that they were simply choosing to be gay to get attention or act out, (because being gay is an easy thing to do in America, right?) have all been proven to be ludicrous arguments against legitimizing gay rights.

I remember, as a kid, hearing the incredibly heartbreaking story of the Matthew Shepard murder, and even then I wondered why people could be so full of hatred and bigotry. Perhaps part of my empathy comes from being a high school band nerd: sure, life wasn't great in high school, but the best thing about high school is that it ends. You get to leave peoples' judgments behind. But for the longest time this hasn't been true for gay people: they were forced to exist in a life-long sort of semi-high school oppression, where they were denied the basic right to marry their partner, because American society didn't approve of that lifestyle.

Sentencing innocent people to a life-long, single existence, and refusing to recognize their basic right to marry, and live a full life, is just incredibly inexcusable and sad. Denying gay rights has led to far too many suicides, police brutality incidents, and other unnecessary pain and suffering for people who simply have a different sexual preference from "the norm." I stand up for this not because I am gay myself, but I do have several gay friends who I believe deserve an equal shot at living happy and fulfilling lives.

Thomas Jefferson wrote a pretty revolutionary document in 1776, that I think most of us are familiar with. There is a passage in the first paragraph that reads: "We hold these truths to be self-evident, that all men [and women] are created equal, that they are endowed by their Creator with certain unalienable Rights, that among these are Life, Liberty and the pursuit of Happiness." Is the freedom to marry, for all men and women, regardless of sexual orientation, not guaranteed by this line? Is marriage not the height of the pursuit of happiness in a romantic relationship?

All relevant marriage jokes aside, the Declaration of Independence, along with the Bill of Rights, sought to establish freedom for Americans to live as they desired: the freedom of speech, of assembly, of the press, to practice whichever religion one wishes to; why should marriage between two consenting adults be excluded? Every argument against gay marriage has been refuted, based on either those, or the basic separation of Church and State. It's time to stop denying these Americans one of the most basic rights of human life, and pass a federal law upholding the right for heterosexual and same-sex couples to marry and be recognized equally. And of course, any employment-related discrimination is equally unconscionable as well.

Edward Snowden

"Few men are willing to brave the disapproval of their peers, the censure of their colleagues, the wrath of their society. Moral courage is a rarer commodity than bravery in battle or great intelligence. Yet it is the one essential, vital quality for those who seek to change a world that yields most painfully to change."
— Robert F. Kennedy

This issue is close to my heart too, for different reasons. There has been a long debate going on about what Edward Snowden, and consequently Glenn Greenwald are, in the wake of their NSA revelations: traitors, heroes, or something in between? I am fully in the hero camp: without those revelations, there is no way we would be having the serious discussions about reform we are having now. And with Guantanamo Bay still open, with alleged enemies of the state being held without a trial, as threats to national security, can you blame Snowden for wanting to do it in the manner he has chosen? Even worse, what does it say about the state of whistleblower protections in the United States, that he felt more comfortable making these revelations from Hong Kong, and sought asylum in Russia, two nations we certainly have tenuous relationships with, at best?

The other ridiculous notion is that Snowden is simply looking for attention, and not acting out of patriotic duty: to that I say, does a young man without a college degree, making $200,000 as an analyst, with a comfortable life in Hawaii and a girlfriend, have anything to lose? He chose to sacrifice all of this, and to basically accept fugitive status, by refusing to be a part of a system that he knew the American people would not approve of, if they understood the scary depths that it went to in order to invade their privacy. If he spends one minute in an American prison cell, it would be a national tragedy.

Daniel Ellsberg, who leaked the Pentagon Papers and went through a similar battle, both in the legal system and the court of

American public opinion, was acquitted of any criminal charges, and by his brave action to disclose those documents effectively led to the end of the Vietnam War. He is widely-celebrated as a hero who, out of moral conviction, knew he could not stay complicit and silent about the sort of defense intelligence that he had seen. To continue to be keep it from the eyes of the American people, who deserved to know the truth about Vietnam, simply felt irresponsible.

I have similar praise to deliver in defense of Julian Assange, Chelsea Manning, and those who attempt to bring transparency in a world full of public relations talking points and corporate agenda-focused news. These figures are not the new Julius and Ethel Rosenberg: they are not selling secrets to our international enemies for private gain, and they are certainly not traitors to the American State. Legendary transparency advocate and Supreme Court Justice Louis D. Brandeis taught us that "Publicity is justly commended as a remedy for social and industrial diseases. Sunlight is said to be the best of disinfectants; electric light the most efficient policeman." Anyone who disagrees with that sentiment very likely has something to hide.

This method of research and publication is essentially the new investigative journalism: it shows us the anxieties of an empire in decline, and exposes the unvarnished truth about policies we may not ever know about otherwise, all in the name of more justice, more democracy, and more truthful information. The supposed threats to national security have largely been exaggerated by those with power, seeking to quiet would-be whistleblowers. We should not be punishing courageous, patriotic individuals who want to start a public debate over what is being done with the American public's tax money, with very little oversight into those practices. We should be celebrating their efforts and sacrifices, not discussing possible lengths of jail sentences for them.

Income Inequality

Inequality, and the many ways it has bled into American life, might be the defining issue of our time. The average CEO now makes 350 times what an average employee makes in the United States. A minimum wage that has not kept up with inflation now dictates that members of the aptly-labeled "working class" regularly have two jobs, rather than one, to just get by. Only 11% of American workers now have the protection of a union. Rental prices for apartments are through the roof, and young people for the most part aren't buying houses out of an inability to do so, between college loan liabilities and the decline of full-time positions offering benefits and economic security.

On the flip side of things, the wealthy have never had it better. The capital gains tax rate of 15% ensures that the highest earners will pay less of a portion of their earnings back to the government than most middle-income Americans. The most profitable American corporations often dodge paying income taxes by basing their operations overseas. The Wall Street firms that colluded to cause the housing bubble and ensuing 2008 collapse of the economy have been allowed to operate largely without prosecution, often paying marginal fines that don't even equate to a drop in the bucket for them. But the golden parachutes are preserved, and the 8-figure executive bonuses are still given.

Matt Taibbi has done the best work documenting the depths of American inequality, from our variable incomes, to those who get jailed for minor infractions, and to those who walk away after committing big white collar ones. French economist Thomas Piketty has argued for a worldwide income tax rate, which may solve some of these issues, but would be difficult to implement too. Clearly, things sound bleak; but there are ways forward. Raising the national minimum wage to $10 an hour would be a good start; $15 would be better.

To those who say that fast food workers aren't worth $15 an hour, I would ask them to observe that job, and watch the non-stop flow of traffic, the handling of money, the pressure to get orders right the first time, quickly, all while working a full shift on your feet. And to those who say that raising the minimum wage would kill jobs: if someone is paid enough to work just one job, and quit the one or possibly two that they currently have in addition to their main one, does that not also open up those positions that are left, due to no longer needed? Wouldn't this create more room in the labor market? I think most consumers would be more than willing to pay a few extra cents if it meant that the workers who serve us, who work so hard for so little, get to have more comfortable lives for themselves and those who depend on them.

In a time when unions are struggling to survive, corporations have largely broken Henry Ford's famous promise, to pay workers enough that they can consume the products that American companies have to sell. This was best pointed out by Robert Reich in his documentary *Inequality for All*, a movie that everyone should see as soon as possible if they haven't yet. Once employers fail to live up to this basic formerly-assumed tenet of employment, the federal government must step in to assure citizens a fair shot at affording the cost of living in an increasingly-more-expensive American marketplace.

Foreign Policy

The issues that face America abroad are certainly diverse and somewhat terrifying. Bashar al-Assad in Syria must be taken seriously; I believe he poses a unique threat to stability in the region because he has the power of the Syrian military behind him, unlike the other Middle Eastern dictators who fell during the Arab Spring to protests. Arming the Syrian rebels is I think the correct move, but we must follow through in our commitment to them. ISIS is a force that we must address, but the nature of the organization makes it difficult to combat effectively. I can say one thing for certain: I am tired of listening to the Bush people complain about how Obama has mishandled the situation. None of this friction would be occurring if Iraq hadn't been senselessly destabilized in the first place.

The road ahead is not totally clear, but I don't believe anyone thinks a prolonged ground troop war is anything that America, or its military and veterans, can handle right now, after all we have asked of them in Iraq and Afghanistan. I do not promote isolationism, but we must be much more careful about where we get involved now: the cost in money and lives is simply too much without a very justified cause. War needs to become much more of a last resort than it has been: is diplomacy not a good thing?

Religion and Violence

There has been some discussion about the seemingly violent-nature of Islam lately. My feeling is that while we see and hear a lot about this, the reality is that most Muslims are peaceful people who wish to live their lives in the same way that other religious people do. But I am not going to disagree that some very unfortunate acts have been committed in the name of religion. I am Catholic, but I cringe to think of some of the atrocities that were committed during the Spanish Inquisition in the 15th century. Religion, in some ways, can be a lot like technology: it can be used by people to do great good, or used to justify great evil. America is a place where all religions and other philosophies are allowed to exist side-by-side, and any persecution based on religious or ethnic group identification should be vehemently condemned. The right to peaceable assembly is too vital to the American way of life to risk limiting it in any unnecessary way.

Gun Control

Gun control is always a touchy subject, and honestly I have mixed feelings in some ways. I have friends who shoot for recreation, and friends who hunt, and I fully support them to engage in their hobbies. I also believe that concealed carry is a lawful practice if it is done after being certified. But there is an obvious need to figure out how to keep our schools and universities safe from senseless acts of violence. There is no easy answer to this, but students and teachers need to feel safe in the classroom and on campus. When a measure like increased background check depth has 90% support and no progress is made, there is something seriously wrong, after so many heartbreaking school shootings have taken place. No gun control law will be perfect, but if it prevents even one more school shooting, would it not be worth it?

Ferguson and Race Relations

The unfortunate situation that unfolded in Ferguson, Missouri this summer told us a lot that we maybe didn't want to hear about race relations in America. It's even more troubling that it occurred so quickly after the tragic murder of Trayvon Martin. But, Ferguson brought to light the reality that a lot of black communities are faced with profiling tactics by white police officers, who typically do not live in that same community. Mistakes happen, but some, like the one that happened to Michael Brown, are simply indefensible. The racial double standards that exist in law enforcement today must be ended. The cruel and unusual "stop-and-frisk" policy pursued by New York City police officers is an unbelievably racist practice that simply needs to stop. Diversity in local police departments seems to be the best solution, as it has shown to prevent abuses and mistakes like the ones we saw in Ferguson.

Recent Immigration Trends

The recent immigration crisis along the Mexico border, which has involved tens of thousands of children from throughout Latin America lining up, hoping to be admitted into the US, has rekindled discussions about America's place in the world in regards to who gets to stay, and who has to leave, when it comes to immigration policies. Immigration quotas have become tighter and tighter since the 1980s, but we as a nation must remember our ancestors' humble roots as immigrants looking for a new start too. Laws are not made to be broken, of course. But there must be an acknowledgment that most recent immigrants do a lot of hard work in industries that have difficulty attracting native-born Americans to complete it.

I am reminded of Emma Lazarus's poem, "The New Colossus," that is emblazoned at the feet of the Statue of Liberty: "...A mighty woman with a torch, whose flame is the imprisoned lightning, and her name Mother of Exiles. From her beacon-hand glows world-wide welcome... 'Give me your tired, your poor, your huddled masses yearning to breathe free, the wretched refuse of your teeming shore. Send these, the homeless, tempest-tost to me, I lift my lamp beside the golden door!'" Once this stops being a welcoming destination for those seeking a new and better life, we fail to be continue the spirit of what America has stood for ever since its colonization began.

Stephen Colbert offered his support for the United Farm Workers in a 2010 Congressional Hearing, and I think his thoughts on the immigration issue are important to consider as well: "I like talking about people who don't have any power, and it seems like one of the least powerful people in the United States are migrant workers, who come in and do our work, but don't have any rights as a result. And yet, we still ask them to come here, and at the same time, ask them to leave. And that's an interesting contradiction to me." We should respect everyone's labor, and I think with this specific group, acknowledge their contribution to America, and that they perform a much-needed service, while seeking a better life in a place we gladly call "The Land of Opportunity."

Global Warming

Global warming is officially real, dangerous, and needs to be treated as a top-tier political issue going forward. The next President must be willing to address this as a real threat to our international well-being. It is time to stop stifling the green energy effort in our transition from oil and gas. The consequences of ignoring this threat are simply too great to flirt with: flooding, more extreme weather, more frequency of natural disasters, wildfires, drought, and possible famine are all very real possibilities. Companies who lead the way in transitioning to solar and wind energy solutions should be rewarded with tax breaks; Americans who choose to drive electric or flex-fuel cars should also receive credits for doing so. We can all do a little bit to make this situation better, and we're all in it together: there is a responsible and sustainable way forward that will make the world a better place for everyone involved.

Marijuana Legalization

The legalization of marijuana came as sort of a surprise last year, from the states of Washington and Colorado. I have sort of mixed feelings about it all: I don't think weed will save the world, but I think with the proof that it can be used medicinally for many purposes, there will be growing acceptance that it may be useful; at least less harmful than hard alcohol and possibly cigarettes. A lot of its future will depend on how the efforts in Colorado and Washington unfold. I believe the legalization argument will start to look like those involving gaming expansion and casinos; it may not be the cleanest way for a state to make additional revenues, but it may be somewhat harmless as well. A vice tax is always more popular than raising other types of taxes; states with budget shortfalls may be increasingly tempted to take the risk and see if the marijuana industry can work for them.

But this isn't the end of the financial advantage to legalizing, or at least decriminalizing, the possession or use of small amounts of marijuana. It would, without question, ease the public expense of arresting, prosecuting, and housing non-violent offenders in an overcrowded prison system. And maybe most important for the international community, it would decrease the violence in Mexico and Central America that we generate with our demand for illegal substances like marijuana, which are trafficked by gangs and other elements that have made those areas, and the Mexican border, so dangerous over the past three years. Still wonder why the Hispanic refugee children came north, to us, to escape the violence? The new legal marijuana industry has also been a job creator in terms of small businesses sprouting up in Colorado and Washington. It could be an important policy reversal that would improve a lot of peoples' situations, without much harm done.

Campaign Finance Reform

Campaign finance reform is always the go-to point for political science professors and people who really understand the problems that big money in politics causes. Democracy really does start to turn into oligarchy when the Kochs, or Sheldon Adelson, can write a $10 million check and exert so much influence over the benefitting politician or PAC that receives it.

A recent Princeton University study actually found that America behaves more like an oligarchy than a democracy now, which is bad, but not surprising, news. The Founding Fathers understood the problem that when the wealthy also have too much political power, they completely run the country. This is how you get income inequality exploding, and the revolving DC-Wall Street door that never seems to stop spinning anymore (right, Eric Cantor?). The McCutcheon ruling has only made matters worse than they were. Al Franken and others are leading the effort for an amendment to rein in big money; hopefully it passes sometime in the next 20 years. Justice Louis Brandeis, in an encore appearance: "We can have democracy in this country, or we can have great wealth concentrated in the hands of a few, but we can't have both."

Voter Suppression

Voter suppression, ranging from a whole range of stupid tricks and tactics, such as manufactured long-wait lines, pointless voter ID laws requiring state-issued IDs, rather than using the standard voter signature for identity verification, which has was always worked fine for the four elections I've served as a judge during, to state-enacted limits on early voting, will all be pursued this year by mainly the Republican Party, as so happens in every big election year. Any attempt to prevent voters from turning out to the polls is absolutely despicable and should be condemned by everyone who supports free and fair elections. Our biggest problem is not that too many citizens in America are voting, but too few. Anyone who witnesses intimidation should feel free to confront it and protest it openly; this is one of our few rights as citizens, making our voices heard every two years, and it should not be abridged by any party.

Related to this, I pose a question to the powers that be: How far are we from online voting in elections? We pay bills online, register to vote online, and buy tons of products on the Internet. I know the tech-savvy Lieutenant Governor of California, Gavin Newsom, agrees with me: our government is stuck in the 1990s in terms of technology, while everyone else lives in the 21st century. If not that, how about at least a national holiday for midterm and general elections? No one would complain. Well, at least no one that loves democratic freedom...

Women and Minorities in American Politics

Finally, I want to close this section with a look at some of the midterm race data. Politics has been an old (white) boys' club for a long, long time now, but I wanted to see if things have gotten any better lately. I did some basic math and found that out of 145 candidates running for Governor or the US Senate this year, largely considered to be the marquis, high-powered offices of the midterms, only 24 candidates are women. That's a very low, staggeringly dismal 16.5% representation of the fairer sex competing for higher offices this year. Obviously we have a long way to come if we want anything resembling proportional representation (50% would probably be a better number). The reasons for this vary, but one of which is that the Parties are often low on recruiting female candidates, which needs to change. Susan Collins, Kelly Ayotte, Kirsten Gillibrand, Elizabeth Warren, and Tammy Baldwin are just a handful of examples of women making a big impact in the US Senate today.

The numbers are even worse for non-white minority candidates: in this group I included African Americans, Hispanics, and those of Asian, Middle-Eastern, and Indian descent. That number came in at a disheartening 14 out of 145; only 9.7% of candidates for these offices are non-white. For as much as we celebrate diversity in America, the Governor's Mansions and Senate Offices are both incredibly Caucasian and male. One thing might be changing though; we're seeing a bit more third-party representation, this year in places like Alaska, South Dakota, and Kansas, but also in Maine and Vermont; all of which might have an Independent representing them in a high-profile seat, after measured dissatisfaction with the options for both main parties. Don't watch for an Independent revolution, but in a time when politics change so little, you have to accept small victories sometimes.

Chapter 6

An Open Letter to the Democratic Party:

I'd be willing to bet that if you visit enough retirement homes, you can find 10 people who remember when the Democratic Party stood for something. That time in America when Democrats stood behind workers, and trade unions, and educators, instead of turning their collective backs on those groups until it became time to raise money for campaigns. Yes, there was a time, not that long ago, when civil and human rights meant more to Democrats than fundraising, if you can believe it.

Rather than shut progressives and liberals out of the Party, their voices were tolerated as positive agents for social change. They were the voices that aided African Americans in gaining voting rights, in ending Jim Crow, in opposing the Vietnam War, which eventually helped to bring it to an end. These were the voices that demanded a New Deal, that led movements to establish the Food and Drug Administration, that pushed for an end to child labor, the enactment of the 40 hour work week, and weekends. They won organizing drives for workers in every line of labor to secure a growing middle class, and an open path to the American Dream.

They understood the value that small businesses added to the economy and local communities, and fought to keep the marketplace competitive and fair, rather than allow for big corporate mergers that came to dominate whole industries. They worried less about keeping friends on Wall Street and more about regulating their behavior, to insure that that the American consumer got protected from scams and schemes that only benefit the financial class. They fought for environmental protections of our most precious ecosystems and resources, rather than permitting big polluters to just pay a fine for the damage they do.

They understood the balance between capitalism and democracy is a fragile one, but a great one: if it is managed to promote the freedoms of citizens, and workers, and entrepreneurs, everyone can be a winner in America. They understood the valuable contributions that immigrants make to our country: the hard work that they do so that the middle and upper classes can enjoy comfortable lives, the expansion of our cultural horizons, the visible proof that if America is working correctly, that they too can start at the "bottom" and work their way up to a middle class living that will be there for them. They would agree that women deserve to be paid the same amount as men do for performing the same work, and should have access to all of the medical advancements that allow them to control their own lives.

They would agree that dissention can be more useful to democracy than blind and passionless assent to the agenda of the powerful. That sometimes people need a helping hand, rather than a scolding, for not being able to find work. That profiling and jailing the nation's young black and Latino men for minor "drug offenses" is a poor way to end racism, addiction, and crime. They believed that the wealthy, who benefit the most from the opportunities provided by capitalism in America, should have to pay taxes back into the system that has given them so much, so that those who are less fortunate can have a shot at making a decent living as well.

They understood that our nation's veterans have answered the call of our country's leaders to serve in dangerous foreign wars, and deserve the benefits of health care, job assistance, and educational opportunities afforded to them by the GI Bill. They would view endless war as a poor and unsustainable foreign policy, and limitless spending on the military-industrial complex to be a waste of tax payer dollars, while so many human capital concerns persist in neglect.

They understood that spending public money on educating our youth isn't flushing money down the toilet, but an investment in our future as a competitive global power that must lead the way in protecting human rights, supporting responsible businesses, and exporting technology. They understood that public works projects to repair and upgrade America's infrastructure is good policy, for both citizen safety, and for putting Americans back to work.

They understood that our retired citizens have spent their lives investing in America, and worked hard for their families, and deserve to live a comfortable life after they've made their contributions to society, rather than struggling to pay for basic amenities or prescription drugs. They would understand that gay men and women have spent far too long as second-class citizens in America, and deserve the same workplace protections and opportunities to marry and raise a family as straight citizens do.

But most of all, they understood that America always has the people and the drive to fix things when they're broken; and the cynicism and greed that have infected most of today's Democratic Party need to be conquered if it is to again become the party of progress that Americans can believe in.

Senator Paul Wellstone said that "Politics is not just about power and money games. Politics can be about the improvement of people's lives, about lessening human suffering in our world, and bringing about more peace, and more justice." There could hardly be a better time to remember this than now.

An Open Letter to the Republican Party:

Hi guys (let's face it, most of you are old white guys),

I'm not sure if you knew this, but Abraham Lincoln was actually in the Republican Party! So were Theodore Roosevelt, Dwight Eisenhower, and everyone's favorite, old Richard Nixon. I bring these fellas up because they did things that you guys would probably never do today.

Lincoln put the rights of a huge group of oppressed minorities before the interests of big businessmen in the South. Teddy broke up Standard Oil, which had become a total monopoly in its industry, and was suffocating competition from other firms while it price gouged consumers. Ike got the Interstate Highway System built, and even if it was approved as a defense measure, can you imagine life today without it? Especially the interstate shipping that healthy businesses require to get things delivered on time? And Tricky Dick, well he wasn't perfect, but those hippies forced him to start the Environmental Protection Agency. And you know what? All of these were government actions that have improved Americans' lives.

So when Mitch McConnell filibusters legislation 400 times over a course of 7 years, one of which was the student loan debt relief bill that Elizabeth Warren sponsored, people who are watching start to get a little pissed off, and wonder why you're really in office. This also happens when the Republican House votes 50 times to repeal Obamacare, which is basically the equivalent of pushing a boulder up a hill 50 times, claiming you accomplished something, and then acting like you don't know why it rolls back down the hill.

This sort of behavior isn't really in the historic spirit of the Republican Party. Well, crossing your arms and pouting about losing and stomping your feet is, but there have been times in history, and not even that long ago, when Republicans actually did things to help govern the country effectively. They permitted moderate voices to participate in debates, and turned out to be the voices of reason that occasionally got things done. Even Patron Saint Ronnie Reagan, who supposedly informs your ideology for governing today, raised taxes eleven times during his eight years in office, after realizing they'd been cut too low. The refusal to govern for the American peoples' interests, even after the deregulation of the banking and insurance industries almost caused the world economy to collapse, has been absolutely inexcusable.

When John Boehner, the leader of your Party, has the nerve to stand up and say something so incredibly ignorant and condescending to the American Enterprise Institute about people who are struggling to make ends meet, there reaches a point when self-awareness or shame appear to not be felt at all. I will quote that statement below:

"This idea that has been born, maybe out of the economy over the last couple years, that you know, I really don't have to work. I don't really want to do this. I think I'd rather just sit around. This is a very sick idea for our country. If you wanted something you worked for it," Boehner said, adding, "Trust me, I did it all."

With all due respect, you have no idea, Mr. Boehner, what things are really like in the economy for normal people right now. You don't have to apply for jobs and compete with maybe 10, or maybe 100 people for the same job, because Republicans in Congress refuse to pass a jobs bill, or unemployment benefits, or an infrastructure bill that would create work for Americans.

No, none of this reality or desperation actually touches you, because you make $223,000 a year, have the best healthcare plan in the world (provided by the federal government, mind you), never have to pay for a meal, and are completely satisfied sitting on your hands, leading a do-nothing Congress in doing nothing. If you and House Republicans, who I should note are in the same position as you, but only get $174,000 a year to waste time, are going to continue to have the audacity to refuse to do work on behalf of the American people, then the very least you can do is respect those who do not have the free ride you've been lucky enough to be handed.

A lot of the people you are talking about are working two or three part-time jobs, between 60 and 80 hours per week, and that's if they are lucky enough to have them at all; often working for a minimum wage that is half what it should be, as it has not kept up with inflation since the 1970s, because your Party refuses to discuss raising it to a humane or livable rate.

To make a long story short, the "Party of No" has not always responded to that name. Please come back to the policymaking table and start participating in serious government again. Like it or not, we need you.

Chapter 7

Making Politics Better: Not Impossible!

Anymore, American politics feels more like being forced to talk to your annoying little brother who can't stop bragging about how great he is, and how dumb his opponents are. And of course the worst part is he always tries to shake you down for cash every time you guys have one of your "lovely talks," because hey, he's family right? And you owe it to him to be supportive, even if he's going to put that money towards a bullhorn to scream the same bland, annoying, repetitive messages through you can't escape from, directly into your ear.

Those of you who are remotely involved with politics know what I'm referencing here: those telephone calls, door hangers, and nonstop fundraising emails just don't do what the political class thinks they do. Though, they keep repeating those tactics, so I guess there's a chance people do give in and donate if you annoy them enough times, in a desperation to end the misery. The emails can occasionally be useful too, if current news or a relevant update is included, but at a certain point, once a certain volume threshold is reached, it just starts to seem ridiculous, and people zone out even more.

I'm looking through my inbox right now for June 30, one of the big campaign finance reporting deadlines: I received a total of 63 emails over June 28th, 29th, and 30th, featuring clever titles such as "QUICK!", "Look at this," and "I need you." While these titles sound more like late-night messages from a drunk ex-lover, they aren't really far off from that. Joe Trippi told us the revolution would not be televised. Unfortunately, it's in your inbox, and way more annoying than most of the attack ads the American population sits through every other September and October.

If politicians want to appeal to Millennials, and even just citizens in general, I think having a sense of humor is invaluable. Some of my personal favorite ads are the goofy, fun Paul Wellstone ones for his 1990 Senate run. But most of all, young people want to be respected, just like every other voting group does. They want serious discussions about things like unemployment and college loan relief, and they have a high sense of awareness when it comes to bullshit, just like the "more mature" voters.

I'm not really suggesting a slapstick routine, or a politician standup tour (God help us all), but it's obvious that Jon Stewart, Stephen Colbert, Bill Maher, and John Oliver have big followings because they understand that covering politics and the media can be done in ways that both engage and entertain. And sometimes, you can't help but laugh at some of the shit that happens in politics today anyway. I should mention, the recent news that Jon Stewart almost took over *Meet the Press* instead of Chuck Todd is the signal from establishment media that his approach works, and it is not just relegated to being "entertainment news" anymore. I think Jon made the right choice by staying at *The Daily Show*, but he would have been excellent in the *Meet the Press* role as well.

To summarize, I think Americans hate politics for the same reasons E.J. Dionne claimed they did in the early 90s – false choice between impractical ideologies, and a lack of the ruling class's ability to connect with what voters really want, despite almost constant polling on every subject imaginable. But I think they also hate politics because of the reason Joe Klein mentions in *Politics Lost* – campaigns have become bland, too long, too predictable, too formulaic, and basically just...too consultant-based. It's difficult to ask people to care about politics when the product that is being put out for them is so uninspired and lifeless, most of the time. Creativity definitely counts when you show an ad 200 times in a one-week span.

I do think we are moving away from the cookie cutter ads and bland messaging that bore so many, but it will be a slow process, and consultants will stick with what they can get away with for as long as they can. On some level, you can't blame them: if it stays profitable, there isn't much motive to change. But I hope the movement doesn't settle on phone banking, robocalls, and email barrages, like it has lately. On some level, people do want to be good citizens who vote. But when you beat the life out of them during the campaign, it's hard to blame them for skipping the ballot box on the first Tuesday in November.

Getting Some Depth Back: A Modest Political Science Proposal

In 2013, crotchety asshole and US Senator from Oklahoma, Tom Coburn (R), got something he'd been after for a long time: an amendment that effectively defunded the research grants for Political Science, granted by the National Science Foundation. The rest of the behavioral sciences: Economics, Psychology, and Sociology, were not subject to the ban. It seemed like Grumpy Tom was out for the Political Scientists. But it got through, with the caveat that research involving national security and the economy be possibly approved if it is submitted to the NSF Director, and deemed "important enough to conduct."

This stunt interrupted a lot of important studies; the American Election Study at the University of Michigan, for example. But the amendment got dropped in 2014, after it saw stiff resistance from the rest of the social science community: after all, were they next? This all comes on the heels of a long campaign to generally defund investigative research journalism. Blame it on the corporate takeover of the media, on the decline of newspaper readership, or whatever you wish. Blogs and non-profits have stepped in to pick up some of the slack, but it feels like there should be a more official arm to the opposition research that used to be so common, and still is so important to keeping political and financial power in check.

But where could we find a big group of disgruntled, professionally-trained researchers, who have a distaste for politicians, who also may have been recently shorted their due Congressional funding?

I'm not the first to advocate for this, but if the academic community were to get more involved in doing political opposition research for the public's interest, especially in terms of what politicians have promised while campaigning, against what they have delivered in terms of policy, it's hard to see this being viewed as a "waste of time and money." Political Science departments would obviously be the first place to discuss such research, but there's no reason it couldn't be opened to the other social science and humanities departments as well.

These research reports, which could be released yearly as politician performance reviews, could be designated for public access, and peer-reviewed to guarantee unbiased, neutral evaluation of politics and policy. They could be valuable for voters to consider and reference when heading to the polls. And to those who might complain about a liberal or Democratic Party bias from academia, I would say that most researchers are much less impressed with Democrats than you might think, and there is a premium on producing neutral, professional research, much less than engaging in political partisanship.

Helping to educate citizens from a civic perspective, rather than forcing the public to rely solely on campaign information, might be a good in-road to producing more high-quality material for voters to rely on for making informed voting decisions. This is not to say that current academic political research projects are lacking in worth or importance: I would say the exact opposite, after being more involved with some, and seeing them put to use.

But this seems like a no-brainer, win-win situation for everyone. It could be as simple as a graduate assistantship with funding for conducting such research, or as important as a professor task force committee. Different colleges and universities could be assigned to research legislators in their district, or the state's colleges could divide the work up and blind it so that there's more of a sense of anonymity. My early list of possible guidelines to evaluate officials on include:

Campaign contribution sources

Significant staffing changes

Votes for/against high-impact legislation

Attendance, missed votes

Committees served on

Bills introduced by subject

Bills co-sponsored

Jobs report summary

Scandals or gaffes

Popularity via polling

Total fit for the district

Overall performance rating

This is just a preliminary list, but I think there's some potential for this to be a positive contribution to democracy and American voting. It might even improve the public discourse, and enhance political transparency. So...who's ready to get started?

Conclusion

I guess it's my hope that this little handbook/almanac/guide helped you hate politics a little less, or at least reduced your level of hatred down to annoyance, where I am. Once we as citizens give up on politics, a system designed to serve our interests, there aren't a whole lot of other levers we can pull. It isn't hard to become cynical with how today's system works, or how it fails to. But ultimately, we are the only people with the power to make things better.

And every little action does add up to something special.

We can vote, we can call our Congresspeople and yell at their underpaid staffers (but don't be too mean), we can refuse to support companies that don't align with our values. We can talk politics in coffee shops or bars, we can forward emails, we can protest on the streets and outside of the institutions we're mad at, we can read an article, we can write an article, we can take an interesting class, we can volunteer to help out a local non-profit, and we can donate what we can afford to worthy causes. This is just the beginning of such a list.

If you should find yourself in the voting booth, confused, displeased, or angry on this November 4th, and need some help deciding whose name to punch the little hole next to, I would implore you to vote for the more thoughtful candidate. The candidate who seems more concerned with listening to your interests, and helping people, along with leading them, because they're our public servants: not the other way around.

I leave you in the hands of a man who knew the true meaning of public service, and the power of being an active American citizen:

"Few may have the greatness to bend history itself, but each of us can work to change a small portion of events. It is from numberless diverse acts of courage and belief that human history is shaped. Each time a person stands up for an ideal, or acts to improve the lot of others, or strikes out against injustice, they send forth a tiny ripple of hope, and crossing each other from a million different centers of energy and daring, those ripples build a current which can sweep down the mightiest walls of oppression and resistance."

— Robert F. Kennedy

Acknowledgments

Joe Klein wisely mused at the end of his consultant-critical bestseller *Politics Lost* that it would be nearly impossible to list all of the influences that have contributed to one's political education over the years. But, that doesn't mean it's not worth foolishly trying to do, so here it goes. First off I have to thank my parents, Doug and Jamie, my sister Jacquie, and my Aunt Gleneth, for their endless support of my wanderings through the years. I want to acknowledge the outpouring of good political writing that's been happening since the Bush years and of course before then. It is said that two groups of people head towards a crisis instead of running away from it: our first responders, and our best writers: Glenn Greenwald, Chris Hedges, Matt Taibbi, Thomas Frank, Joseph Stiglitz, Paul Krugman, Rachel Maddow, Keith Olbermann, Jared Bernstein, Robert Reich, Barbara Ehrenreich, E.J. Dionne, Chris Cillizza, Rich Miller, and of course the late Christopher Hitchens have all produced smart, important, and incisive works that I greatly admire. It feels strange to claim a mentor that I haven't yet had the pleasure to meet in person, but Robert Reich's leadership and writing on protecting workers and his analysis of the explosion of American inequality are essentially what compelled me to take to writing for my own causes seriously. Stephen Colbert, Bill Maher, Jon Stewart, and John Oliver all deserve so much credit for making politics into a laughing, but also serious matter, and engaging American viewers and voters who otherwise may not care about politics at all. Art keeps all of us sane: I especially want to say thanks to Lewis Black, Patton Oswalt, Aziz Ansari, Louis CK, Marc Maron, Chris Rock, Trey Parker, Matt Stone, Seth MacFarlane, George Clooney, Oliver Stone, Matt Damon, Eminem, Chris Martin, the Green Day guys, and Rage Against the Machine, for their artistic visions and political work they've done. Some of my fellow Illinois alums I'm especially proud to claim: the late-Roger Ebert, Hugh Hefner, John Corzine, and Shahid Khan have all proven that we Midwestern folk have something of use to say occasionally. A quick nod to some of my favorite teachers and friends: Joe Miller, Dylan Burns, Jack Vuylsteke, Max Kienzler, Pat Kojima, Thomas Cory, Zach Abrams, Joe Torchedlo, Minhao Jiang, Nestor Guerra, Holly Dillemuth, Michael Phelan, Aaron Meyer, Emily Meyer, Charlie Sales, Michelle Boone, Katherine Ferry, Whitney Schlosser, Shilpa Grover, Perry Stamp, Nathan Stamp, Melissa Lydston, Chris Neiweem, Seth Miller, Gene Giannotta, Kendall Cramer, Hamed Aziz, John Perry, Dan Reynolds, Caitlin Brandt, Sasha Bassett, Dan Walker, Peter Rosa, Hannah Gallup, Debbie Miller, Olivia Dorothy, Jake Gephart, Alyssa Ramirez, Kyle VonDeBur, Kate Varvel, Phil Seck, Tom Lavin, Barb Tanzyus, Rebecca Budde, Denise Fuchs, Brother James Lewnard, the late-Kathleen Bawden, Mahesh Grossman, Lynette and Scott Shaw-Smith, Amy Lakin, JoAnna Beth Tweedy, David Logan, Pete Ellertsen, Bob Blankenberger, Barb Tanzyus, Alice Gutierrez, Steve Stowers, Pat Giocomini, Krist Ormand, and Jeff Mueller have all been terrific educators and friends, willing to humor my political ramblings. Christopher Kennedy, Damarys Canache, Kevin McClure, Linda Smith, Allen Renear, Robert Burger, Marten Stromberg, Maria Bonn, John Wilkin, Mary Wilkes-Towner, and Emily Knox from UIUC were wonderful influences and leaders in their respective fields. Tim Johnson and Allyson Holbrook of the UIC Survey Research Center were excellent teachers and outstandingly patient in my quest to make sense of survey research practices. Speaking of surveys, Dick Schuldt, Mark Winland, Gayla Oyler, and Val Howell were excellent supervisors and co-workers at the UIS Survey Research Office. My closure advisor and UIS mentor Calvin Mouw deserves a special thanks for putting up with me in what turned out to be six educationally-rewarding courses. Additionally, John Transue, Michael Miller, Kent Redfield, Christopher Mooney, Charles Good, and Richard Gilman-Opalsky are all responsible for making the UIS Political Science program into one of the true diamonds in the rough of American Political Science education, especially in terms of State and American Politics. Thank you to everyone for your support; if I forgot anyone I apologize, you know who you are.

A Note about Sources

Endnotes will be made available on my personal website, anthonywilcox.com – I did not have a research or editorial assistant, so any errors in citation are my own. I do want to mention some of the great sources available for people interested in tracking politics now.

Some of those that I reviewed in my analysis include Real Clear Politics, Ballotpedia, HuffPost Pollster, OpenSecrets.org, Chris Cillizza's "The Fix" political blog at the *Washington Post*, Rich Miller's "CapitolFax" blog about Illinois politics, Michael Sneed's columns for the *Chicago-Sun Times*, Carolyn Lochhead's work for the *SF Chronicle*, Dan Walters' work for *The Sacramento Bee*, Bernie Schoenburg's analysis for *The State-Journal Register*, Chris Hedges' *Truthdig*, Politifact at the *Tampa Bay Tribune* is terrific for transparency, and *Politico* as always provides great analysis. Matt Taibbi's work in the *Rolling Stone*, and just about everything *Mother Jones* puts out are also indispensable. And of course a nod to *The Guardian* for their fearless reporting of the Snowden revelations.

About the Author

Anthony Wilcox is happy to announce the launch of FairPayNow.org, his political blog dedicated to analyzing labor economics and inequality. Its primary purpose is to publicize and improve the living standard of underpaid, hard-working people everywhere.

He has previously interned for U.S. Senator Dick Durbin in his Capitol Hill office; on the campaign trail in central Illinois for Governor Pat Quinn's winning 2010 bid; with the national polling firm Lake Research Partners, in Berkeley, CA; and in the legislative office for the Communications Workers of America union in Washington, DC. He also worked as a Committee Clerk for the 2012 legislative session at the Illinois House of Representatives. Lest you be led to believe he's just another Democratic Party hack, he has been a registered Republican voter in both the 2012 and 2014 primary elections.

He holds an M.A. in Political Science from the University of Illinois at Springfield, an M.S. in Information Science from the University of Illinois at Urbana-Champaign, and a Certificate in Survey Research Methods from the University of Illinois at Chicago. He is simultaneously both proud and slightly ashamed to be from Springfield, Illinois, the state capital of the Land of Lincoln. He is currently in the San Francisco Bay Area, doing research on his next project. At publication, he remains both a concerned, and annoyed American citizen and voter. You should follow him on Twitter! @anthonytwilcox

www.ingramcontent.com/pod-product-compliance
Lightning Source LLC
Chambersburg PA
CBHW020516290526
45786CB00002B/629

* 9 781502 761552 *